<u>Plain Song</u> by Jim Harrison

T0166364

J.T.Harrison appears to be .... instincts for
where to break his lines, fo........................ xxxxx meanings
beyond appearance yet can if you will be taken for itself alone, for the
sound of words in relation to their meaning. He belongs to a tradition
that includes poets as far apart in time as Sappho and Lorca, Li Po and
much of William Carlos Williams - a tradition of non-didactic, non-philos -
ophizing poetry in which 'form follows function' and symbols are not
applied but are deeply inherent in the image itself - in a word, the purest
lyric tradition, which partakes of the nature of music without imitating it.

He is 26 years old,and lives in Brookline, Mass. , where he drives a
library delivery van. After graduating from college he was a teaching
assistant for a while while working for his M.A., but abandoned the academic
life as he felt it to be in conflict (for him) with the life of poetry.
He is married and has a 4year old daughter. His childhood was spent in
rural Northern Michigan.

When I say he is a'natural'poet I mean, not that he has not had to struggle
and evolve but that after years of hard work he has apparently tapped a well
in himself. At 26 he is ĭxxxxxxxxxymature person and a poet who has
found his own voice. He is unpublished, or virtually so, as he has waited
to send work to magazines until he felt he had reached a stage when he
was ' good enough' - Would there was a little more such modesty around!
I have never met him, but we had talked on the telephone and he did me
the honor of making me the first person (outside, I suppose, one or two
close friends and his wife) to read through the present manuscript. I
think it is a beautiful book.

                    Denise levertov.

Self portrait.

My left eye is blind and jogs like
a milky sparrow in its socket-
~~I thought it a window to rage~~
~~until I found that rage is never cloudy.~~
The nose is large and ~~doesn't~~ *never* flare
in anger- the front teeth are bucked
but not in lechery. I sucked
my thumb until the age of twelve.
My youth was happy I was never lonely.
though my friends called me 'pig eye'
and the teachers thought me loony.
~~I never wander~~
When I bruised my psyche remained intact:
I fell from horses, and once a cow
but never pigs. Our neighbor lost a hand
to a sow.
I feared the salesman ~~of glass~~ eyes
~~their~~ cases full of fishy baubles-
against the black velvet, jeweled gore.
And going to the store for bread
the intricate latches would never yield.
I always slid in behind someone else.
And the ~~pump-arm~~ *black* on oil wells
and the steel teeth on a combineroaring in the sun
electric fences.

From my ancestors the swedes I inherit
the love of rainy woods, kegs of herring
and whiskey. I remember long *nights* ~~winter~~
evenings of pinochole. the rug smelled
faintly of manure and kerosine.
They laughed loudly but sometimes didn't speak
for the days. But from the German Mennonites
I got intolerance, an aimless diligence
I ~~curse~~ *loathe* them now for their ignorance.

this gray smoke prayers
and porky daughters

In 53 a revival came through town
~~and left me holy in its wake.~~
I knelt on a cold register for hours
in search of purity. woke up warm I was baptized
by immersion in the tank a Williamston
The rusty water stung my eyes. The
minister's moronic son giggled
when I took off my clothes. I left
off the old things of the flesh but not for long.

one night beside a lake a girl dried my
feet with her hair. *a cloal event dii*

It loved Jubal
and Peter Hagar

Backslog

Now the self is the first sacrement.
~~and when the sexuals is discovered~~
~~we'll have a new sacred book~~

(*they talk of left & right prelude. !*
who loves not the misery and ran
of present tense - is lost. the stran
for lunar arrogance. Light macerates.
the lamp infects Warm more warmth

It is difficult to imagine these conversations
between Jesus and Buddha going on at this very moment
that repeats itself in every direction infinite times
they could ask Shakespear and Mozart to write words and music,
and perhaps a dozen others, but they have already done so
the vast asteroid on its way to the largo goes unmentioned –

Come down to earth. Get your head out of your ass.
Get your head out of the clouds, ~~Get moving~~
~~Stop and listen~~. Pay attention! Don't set there scratching
your ass. Stop mooning around. Get to work on time.
~~Hurry or you'll miss the flight that kills you~~.
time and tide that wait for no man willingly
pause for the bare armed girl brushing her hair
in a brown pickup truck on a summer evening

If that bald head gets you closer to Buddha
try chemotherapy ~~will work even faster~~. the hair drops
casually to the floor. The eyes widen until the skull aches and
the heart is Chumpei's fool.
You don't need to think of heaven if it's near.
Who knows? Maybe you're the lamb you refused to eat.

I have accepted the fact that I'll never understand
the universe that I saw clearly for the first time
from our roof at nineteen in miniature heaven.
We belonged to each other! Love at first sight
notwithstanding the child staring in fear at the northern
lights, the milky way in convulsive drift.
Now a lone star in the mountain's saddle banishes years of doubt

It wasn't until the sixth century that the Christians
decided animals weren't part of the Kingdom of heaven
Hoof, caring, and paw can't put money in the collection plate
these lunatic shit brained fools excluded our beloved creatures
theologians & economists, the same thing really. But maybe
my irascible new pup is from the lineage of St Paul

JIM HARRISON: THE ESSENTIAL POEMS

BOOKS BY JIM HARRISON

Jim Harrison:

THE ESSENTIAL POEMS

Edited by Joseph Bednarik

COPPER CANYON PRESS
Port Townsend, Washington

Deep bows of gratitude to Dan Gerber and Ted Kooser for their wise counsel during the creation of *Jim Harrison: The Essential Poems*. Thanks also to Hank Meijer and the archivists at Grand Valley State University—the exhaustive Jim Harrison archive is a marvel to behold.

Copyright 2019 by the James T. Harrison Trust

All rights reserved

Printed in the United States of America

Cover art: *Bristlecone Pine & the Milky Way,* www.fredmertzphotography.com

Copper Canyon Press is in residence at Fort Worden State Park in Port Townsend, Washington, under the auspices of Centrum. Centrum is a gathering place for artists and creative thinkers from around the world, students of all ages and backgrounds, and audiences seeking extraordinary cultural enrichment.

LIBRARY OF CONGRESS CATALOGING-IN-PUBLICATION DATA

Names: Harrison, Jim, 1937–2016, author. | Bednarik, Joseph, 1964– editor.
Title: Jim Harrison: The essential poems / edited by Joseph Bednarik.
Description: Port Townsend, Washington : Copper Canyon Press, [2019] |
    Includes indexes.
Identifiers: LCCN 2018049116 | ISBN 9781556595288 (paperback : alk. paper)
Subjects: LCSH: American poetry—20th century. | American poetry—
    21st century.
Classification: LCC PS3558.A67 A6 2019 | DDC 811/.54—dc23
LC record available at https://lccn.loc.gov/2018049116

Copper Canyon Press
Post Office Box 271
Port Townsend, Washington 98368

www.coppercanyonpress.org

MIX
Paper from
responsible sources
FSC
www.fsc.org   FSC® C011935

Jim Harrison: The Essential Poems
is dedicated to the memory of
Linda King Harrison
and to
Jamie Harrison Potenberg
Anna Harrison Hjortsberg
Joyce Harrington Bahle

CONTENTS

IN SEARCH OF SMALL GODS | *2009*

SONGS OF UNREASON | *2011*

Any volume of essential poems is initially measured by a specific kind of astonishment—by what is *not* included, as in:

"Where's 'Outlyer'? Jim Harrison was the *definition* of an outlier, so that genius suite has to be in the *Essential.*"

It may be cold comfort to those particular readers that the suite "In Interims: Outlyer" *was* in the working manuscript until the final cut. As were two dozen other poems, including some personal favorites. Removing four more letters from *Letters to Yesenin* was especially difficult, since that sequence is structured as a month of daily correspondence, and something is most assuredly lost when reading excerpts.

That said, something is most assuredly gained when readers, inspired by what they find in the *Essential,* seek out *Letters to Yesenin* and experience the entire sequence in one sitting. And if you do so, gentle reader, please leave yourself plenty of emotional space and know that a poet saved his life writing that book:

... Today you make me want to tie myself to
a tree, stake my feet to earth herself so I can't get away. It didn't
come as a burning bush or pillar of light but I've decided to stay.

While *staying,* Jim Harrison was a prolific writer: ten more books of poems followed, as well as novels, novellas, nonfiction, food columns, and screenplays. Instead of being a poet who lived in relative obscurity and poverty in rural Michigan, he became a literary legend who preferred rivers and thickets to the halls of any Academy. "Someone has to stay outside," he told the *Los Angeles Times.*

In the poem "Adding It Up," Jim wrote: "I can't help but count out of habit." In honor of his counting habit, the book you hold in your hand is a distillation of nearly 1,000 poems published within fourteen volumes over fifty years. Every poem in this slender volume deserves to be here, for good reason. That said, it is quite likely that some readers will take issue—perhaps passionate issue—with certain and specific poems and lines and words contained herein. With these readers in mind, I bring forward the concluding line from a *New York Times* review from early in Jim's career: "This is poetry worth loving, hating, and fighting over, a subjective mirror of our American days and needs." That insight is as true today as when it appeared in 1971, and *The Essential Poems* stands as testament that Jim Harrison's poetry is worth our fierce attention.

Joseph Bednarik
Port Townsend, Washington

JIM HARRISON: THE ESSENTIAL POEMS

Poetry, at its best, is the language your soul would
speak if you could teach your soul to speak.
—JIM HARRISON, "POETRY AS SURVIVAL"

Plain Song

| 1965

POEM

Form is the woods: the beast,
a bobcat padding through red sumac,
the pheasant in brake or goldenrod
that he stalks—both rise to the flush,
the brief low flutter and catch in air;
and trees, rich green, the moving of boughs
and the separate leaf, yield
to conclusions they do not care about
or watch—the dead, frayed bird,
the beautiful plumage,
the spoor of feathers
and slight, pink bones.

SKETCH FOR A JOB-APPLICATION BLANK

My left eye is blind and jogs like
a milky sparrow in its socket;
my nose is large and never flares
in anger, the front teeth, bucked,
but not in lechery—I sucked
my thumb until the age of twelve.
O my youth was happy and I was never lonely
though my friends called me "pig eye"
and the teachers thought me loony.

(When I bruised, my psyche kept intact:
I fell from horses, and once a cow but never
pigs—a neighbor lost a hand to a sow.)

But I had some fears:
the salesman of eyes,
his case was full of fishy baubles,
against black velvet, jeweled gore,
the great cocked hoof of a Belgian mare,
a nest of milk snakes by the water trough,
electric fences,
my uncle's hounds,
the pump arm of an oil well,
the chop and whir of a combine in the sun.

From my ancestors, the Swedes,
I suppose I inherit the love of rainy woods,
kegs of herring and neat whiskey –
I remember long nights of pinochle,
the bulge of Redman in my grandpa's cheek;
the rug smelled of manure and kerosene.

They laughed loudly and didn't speak for days.

(But on the other side, from the German Mennonites,
their rag-smoke prayers and porky daughters
I got intolerance, and aimless diligence.)

In '51 during a revival I was saved:
I prayed on a cold register for hours
and woke up lame. I was baptized
by immersion in the tank at Williamston –
the rusty water stung my eyes.
I left off the old things of the flesh
but not for long—one night beside a pond
she dried my feet with her yellow hair.
O actual event dead quotient
cross become green
I still love Jubal but pity Hagar.

(Now self is the first sacrament
who loves not the misery and taint
of the present tense is lost.
I strain for a lunar arrogance.
Light macerates
the lamp infects
warmth, more warmth, I cry.)

NORTHERN MICHIGAN

On this back road the land
has the juice taken out of it:

stump fences surround nothing
worth their tearing down

by a deserted filling station
a Veedol sign, the rusted hulk

of a Frazer, "live bait"
on battered tin.

        A barn
with half a tobacco ad
owns the greenness of a manure
pile

a half-moon on a privy door
a rope swinging from an elm. A

collapsed henhouse, a pump
with the handle up

the orchard with wild tangled branches.

      —

In the far corner of the pasture,
in the shadow of the woodlot
a herd of twenty deer:
                three bucks
are showing off –

they jump in turn across the fence,
flanks arch and twist to get higher
in the twilight
as the last light filters
through the woods.

FAIR/BOY CHRISTIAN TAKES A BREAK

This other speaks of bones, blood-wet
and limber, the rock in bodies. He takes
me to the slaughterhouse, where lying
sprawled, as a giant coil of rope,
the bowels of cattle. At the county fair
we pay an extra quarter to see the her-
maphrodite. We watch the secret air tube
blow up the skirts of the farm girls,
tanned to the knees then strangely white.
We eat spareribs and pickled eggs,
the horses tear the ground to pull a load
of stone; in a burning tent we see
Fantasia do her Love Dance with the
Spaniard—they glisten with sweat, their
limbs knot together while below them farm
boys twitter like birds. Then the breasts
of a huge Negress rotate to a march in
opposing directions, and everyone stamps
and cheers, the udders shine in blurring
speed. Out of the tent we pass produce
stalls, some hung with ribbons, squash
and potatoes stacked in pyramids. A buck-
toothed girl cuts her honorable-mention
cake; when she leans to get me water
from a milk pail her breasts are chaste.
Through the evening I sit in the car (the
other is gone) while my father watches
the harness race, the 4-H talent show.
I think of St. Paul's Epistles and pray
the removal of what my troubled eyes have seen.

LISLE'S RIVER

Dust followed our car like a dry brown cloud.
At the river we swam, then in the canoe passed
downstream toward Manton; the current carried us
through cedar swamps, hot fields of marsh grass
where deer watched us and the killdeer shrieked.
We were at home in a thing that passes.
And that night, camped on a bluff, we ate eggs
and ham and three small trout; we drank too much
whiskey and pushed a burning stump down the bank –
it cast hurling shadows, leaves silvered and darkened,
the crash and hiss woke up a thousand birds.

Now, tell me, other than lying between some woman's legs,
what joy have you had since, that equaled this?

DEAD DEER

Amid pale green milkweed, wild clover,
a rotted deer
curled, shaglike,
after a winter so cold
the trees split open.
I think she couldn't keep up with
the others (they had no place
to go) and her food,
frozen grass and twigs,
wouldn't carry her weight.

Now from bony sockets,
she stares out on this
cruel luxuriance.

Locations

| 1968

WALKING

Walking back on a chill morning past Kilmer's Lake
into the first broad gully, down its trough
and over a ridge of poplar, scrub oak, and into
a larger gully, walking into the slow fresh warmth
of midmorning to Spider Lake where I drank
at a small spring remembered from ten years back;
walking northwest two miles where another gully
opened, seeing a stump on a knoll where my father
stood one deer season, and tiring of sleet and cold
burned a pine stump, the snow gathering fire-orange
on a dull day; walking past charred stumps blackened
by the '81 fire to a great hollow stump near a basswood
swale—I sat within it on a November morning
watching deer browse beyond my young range of shotgun
and slug, chest beating hard for killing –
into the edge of a swale waist-high with ferns,
seeing the quick movement of a blue racer,
and thick curl of the snake against a birch log,
a pale blue with nothing of the sky in it,
a fleshy blue, blue of knotted veins in an arm;
walking to Savage's Lake where I ate my bread
and cheese, drank cool lake water, and slept for a while,
dreaming of fire, snake and fish and women in white
linen walking, pinkish warm limbs beneath white linen;
then walking, walking homeward toward Well's Lake,
brain at boil now with heat, afternoon glistening
in yellow heat, dead dun-brown grass, windless,
with all distant things shimmering, grasshoppers, birds
dulled to quietness; walking a log road near a cedar swamp
looking cool with green darkness and whine of mosquitoes,
crow's caw overhead, Cooper's hawk floating singly

in mateless haze; walking dumbly, footsore, cutting
into evening through sumac and blackberry brambles,
onto the lake road, feet sliding in the gravel,
whippoorwills, night birds wakening, stumbling to lake
shore, shedding clothes on sweet moss; walking
into syrupy August moonless dark, water cold, pushing
lily pads aside, walking out into the lake with feet
springing on mucky bottom until the water flows overhead;
sinking again to walk on the bottom then buoyed up,
walking on the surface, moving through beds of reeds,
snakes and frogs moving, to the far edge of the lake
then walking upward over the basswood and alders, the field
of sharp stubble and hay bales, toward the woods,
floating over the bushy crests of hardwoods and tips
of pine, barely touching in miles of rolling heavy dark,
coming to the larger water, there walking along the troughs
of waves folding in upon themselves; walking to an island,
small, narrow, sandy, sparsely wooded, in the middle
of the island in a clump of cedars a small spring
which I enter, sliding far down into a deep cool
dark endless weight of water.

SUITE TO FATHERS

for Denise Levertov

I

I think that night's our balance,
our counterweight—a blind woman
we turn to for nothing but dark.

—

In Val-Mont I see a slab of parchment,
a black quill pen in stone.
In a sculptor's garden
there was a head made from stone,
large as a room, the eyes neatly hooded
staring out with a crazed somnolence
fond of walled gardens.

—

The countesses arch like cats in châteaux.
They wake up as countesses and usually sleep with counts.
Nevertheless he writes them painful letters,
thinking of Eleanor of Aquitaine, Gaspara Stampa.
With Kappus he calls forth the stone in the rose.

—

In Egypt the dhows sweep the Nile
with ancient sails. I am in Egypt,
he thinks, this Baltic jew—it is hot,
how can I make bricks with no straw?
His own country rich with her food and slaughter,
fit only for sheep and generals.

—

He thinks of the coffin of the East,
of the tiers of dead in Venice,
those countless singulars.
At lunch, the baked apple too sweet with kirsch
becomes the tongues of convent girls at gossip,
under the drum and shadow of pigeons
the girl at promenade has almond in her hair.

—

From Duino, beneath the mist,
the green is so dark and green it cannot bear itself.
In the night, from black paper
I cut the silhouette of this exiled god,
finding him as the bones of a fish in stone.

II

In the cemetery the grass is pale,
fake green as if dumped from Easter baskets,
from overturned clay and the deeper marl
which sits in wet gray heaps by the creek.
There are no frogs, death drains there.
Landscape of glass, perhaps Christ
will quarry you after the worms.
The newspaper says caskets float in leaky vaults.
Above me, I feel paper birds.
The sun is a brass bell.
This is not earth I walk across
but the pages of some giant magazine.

—

Come song,
allow me some eloquence,
good people die.

—

The June after you died
I dove down into a lake,
the water turned to cold, then colder,
and ached against my ears.
I swam under a sunken log then paused,
letting my back rub against it,
like some huge fish with rib cage
and soft belly open to the bottom.
I saw the light shimmering far above
but did not want to rise.

—

It was so far up from the dark –
once it was night three days,
after that four, then six and over again.
The nest was torn from the tree,
the tree from the ground,
the ground itself sinking torn.
I envied the dead their sleep of rot.
I was a fable to myself,
a speech to become meat.

III

Once in Nevada I sat on a boulder at twilight –
I had no ride and wanted to avoid the snakes.
I watched the full moon rise a fleshy red
out of the mountains, out of a distant sandstorm.
I thought then if I might travel deep enough
I might embrace the dead as equals,
not in their separate stillness as dead, but in music
one with another's harmonies.

The moon became paler,
rising, floating upward in her arc
and I with her, intermingled in her whiteness,
until at dawn again she bloodied
herself with earth.

—

In the beginning I trusted in spirits,
slight things, those of the dead in procession,
the household gods in mild delirium
with their sweet round music and modest feasts.
Now I listen only to that hard black core,
a ball harsh as coal, rending for light
far back in my own sour brain.

—

The tongue knots itself
a cramped fist of music,
the oracle a white-walled room of bone
that darkens now with a greater dark;
and the brain a glacier of blood,
inching forward, sliding, the bottom
silt covered but sweet,
becoming a river now
laving the skull with coolness —
the leaves on her surface
dipping against the bone.

—

Voyager, the self the voyage —
dark, let me open your lids.
Night stares down with her great bruised eye.

LULLABY FOR A DAUGHTER

Go to sleep. Night is a coal pit
full of black water –
    night's a dark cloud
full of warm rain.

Go to sleep. Night is a flower
resting from bees –
    night's a green sea
swollen with fish.

Go to sleep. Night is a white moon
riding her mare –
    night's a bright sun
burned to black cinder.

Go to sleep,
night's come,
cat's day,
owl's day,
star's feast of praise,
moon to reign over
her sweet subject, dark.

LOCATIONS

I want this hardened arm to stop
dragging a cherished image.
RIMBAUD

In the end you are tired of those places,
you're thirty, your only perfect three,
you'll never own another thing.
At night you caress them as if the tongue
turned inward could soothe, head lolling
in its nest of dark, the heart fibrotic,
inedible. Say that on some polar night
an Eskimo thinks of his igloo roof, the blocks
of ice sculptured to keep out air, as the roof
of his skull; all that he is, has seen,
is pictured there—thigh with the texture
of the moon, whale's tooth burnished from use
as nothing, fixtures of place, some delicate
as a young child's ear, close as snails to earth,
beneath the earth as earthworms, farther beneath
as molten rock, into the hollow, vaulted place,
pure heat and pure whiteness,
where earth's center dwells.

You were in Harar but only for a moment,
rifles jostling blue barrels against blue barrels
in the oxcart, a round crater, hot, brown,
a bowl of hell covered with dust.

The angels you sensed in your youth
smelled strongly as a rattlesnake
smells of rotten cucumber, the bear

rising in the glade of ferns of hot fur
and sweat, dry ashes pissed upon.

You squandered your time as a mirror,
you kept airplanes from crashing at your doorstep,
they lifted themselves heavily to avoid your sign,
fizzling like matches in the Atlantic.

You look at Betelgeuse for the splendor
of her name but she inflames another universe.
Our smallest of suns barely touches earth
in the Gobi, Sahara, Mojave, Mato Grosso.

Dumb salvages: there is a box made of wood,
cavernous, all good things are kept there,
and if the branches of ice that claw against the window
become hands, that is their business.

Yuma is an unbearable place.
The food has fire in it as
does the brazero's daughter
who serves the food in an orange dress
the color of a mussel's lip.
Outside it is hot as the crevasse
of her buttocks—perfect body temperature.
You have no idea where your body stops
and the heat begins.

On Lake Superior the undertow swallows
a child and no one notices until evening.
They often drown in the green water
of abandoned gravel pits,
or fall into earth where the crust is thin.

I have tried to stop the war.

You wanted to be a sculptor
creating a new shape that would exalt itself
as the shape of a ball or hand
or breast or dog or hoof,
paw print in snow, each cluster of grapes
vaguely diffcrent, bat's wing shaped
as half a leaf, a lake working
against its rim of ground.

You wear yellow this year for Christmas,
the color of Christ's wounds after three days,
the color of Nelse's jacket you wear when writing,
Nelse full of Guckenheimer, sloth, herring, tubercles.

There were sweet places to sleep: beds warmed
by women who get up to work or in the brush
beneath Coit Tower, on picnic tables in Fallon, Nevada,
and Hastings, Nebraska, surrounded by giant curs,
then dew that falls like fine ice upon your face
in a bean field near Stockton, near a waterfall
in the Huron Mountains, memorable sleeps
in the bus stations of San Jose and Toledo, Ohio.

At a roller rink on Chippewa Lake
the skaters move to calliope music.
You watch a motorboat putt by the dock,
they are trolling for bass at night
and for a moment the boat and the two men
are caught in the blue light of the rink,
then pass on slowly upon the black water.

Liquor has reduced you to thumbnails,
keratin, the scales of fish
your ancient relatives,
stranded in a rock pool.

O claritas, sweet suppleness
of breath,
love within a cloud that
blinds us
hear, speak, the world without.

Grove St., Gough St., Heber, Utah,
one in despair, two in disgust,
the third beneath the shadow
of a mountain wall, beyond
the roar of a diesel truck,
faintly the screech of lion.

Self-immolation,
the heaviest of dreams —
you become a charcoal rick
for Christ, for man himself.
They laugh with you as you disappear
lying as a black log upon the cement,
the fire doused by your own blood.

The thunderstorm moved across the lake
in a sheet of rain, the lightning
struck a strawpile, which burned in the night
with hot roars of energy
as in '48 when a jet plane crashed near town,
the pilot parachuting as a leaf through the red sky,
landing miles away, missing the fire.

There was one sun,
one cloud,
two horses running,
a leopard in chase;
only the one sun and a single cloud
a third across her face.
Above, the twelve moons of Jupiter
hissing in cold and darkness.

You worshiped the hindquarters
of beautiful women,
and the beautiful hindquarters of women
who were not beautiful;
the test was the hindquarters
as your father judged cattle.

He is standing behind a plow
in a yellow photograph,
a gangster hat to the back of his head,
in an undershirt with narrow straps,
reins over a shoulder waiting for the photo,
the horses with a foreleg raised,
waiting for the pull with impatience.

The cannon on the courthouse lawn was plugged,
useless against the japs.

In the dark barn
a stillborn calf on the straw,
rope to hooves, its mother bawling
pulled nearly to death.

You've never been across the ocean,
you swept the auditorium with a broom

after the travel lectures and dreamed of going
but the maps have become old, the brain
set on the Mackenzie River, even Greenland
where dentists stalk polar bears from Cessnas.

The wrecked train smelled of camphor,
a bird floating softly above the steam,
the door of the refrigerator car cracked open
and food begins to perish in the summer night.

You've become sure that every year
the sky descends a little,
but there is joy in this pressure,
joy bumping against the lid
like a demented fly, a bird breaking
its neck against a picture window
while outside new gods roll over
in the snow in billowy sleep.

The oil workers sit on the curb
in front of the Blue Moon Bar & Cafe,
their necks red from the sun,
pale white beneath the collars
or above the sleeves; in the distance
you hear the clumping of the wells.
And at a friend's house
there are aunts and uncles, supper plates
of red beans and pork, a guitar is taken
from the wall—in the music
the urge of homesickness, a peach not to be held
or a woman so lovely but not to be touched,
some former shabby home far south of here,
in a warmer place.

Cold cement, a little snow upon it.
Where are the small gods who bless cells?
There are only men. Once you were in a room
with a girl of honey-colored hair,
the yellow sun streamed down air of yellow straw.
You owe it to yourself to despise this place,
the walls sift black powder;
you owe yourself a particular cave.
You wait for her, a stone in loamy stillness,
who will arrive with less pitiful secrets
from sidereal reaches, from other planets of the mind,
who beneath the chamber music of gown and incense
will reflect the damp sweetness of a cave.

At that farm there were so many hogs,
in the center of the pen in the chilled air
he straddles the pig and slits its throat,
blood gushes forth too dark to be blood,
gutted, singed, and scraped into pinkness –
there are too many bowels, the organs
too large, pale sponges that are lungs,
the pink is too pink to understand.

This is earth I've fallen against,
there was no life before this;
                    still icon
as if seen through mist,
cold liquid sun, blue falling
from the air,
                    foam of ship's prow
cutting water, a green shore beyond
the rocks;
beyond, a green continent.

Outlyer & Ghazals

| 1971

DRINKING SONG

I want to die in the saddle. An enemy of civilization
I want to walk around in the woods, fish and drink.

I'm going to be a child about it and I can't help it, I was
born this way and it makes me very happy to fish and drink.

I left when it was still dark and walked on the path to the
river, the Yellow Dog, where I spent the day fishing and drinking.

After she left me and I quit my job and wept for a year and
all my poems were born dead, I decided I would only fish and drink.

Water will never leave earth and whiskey is good for the brain.
What else am I supposed to do in these last days but fish and drink?

In the river was a trout, and I was on the bank, my heart in my
chest, clouds above, she was in NY forever and I, fishing and drinking.

GHAZALS

I

Unbind my hair, she says. The night is white and warm,
the snow on the mountains absorbing the moon.

We have to get there before the music begins, scattered,
elliptical, needing to be drawn together and sung.

They have dark green voices and listening, there are birds,
coal shovels, the glazed hysteria of the soon-to-be-dead.

I suspect Jesus *will* return and the surprise will be
fatal. I'll ride the equator on a whale, a giraffe on land.

Even stone when inscribed bears the ecstatic. Pressed to
some new wall, ungiving, the screams become thinner.

Let us have the tambourine and guitars and forests, fruit,
and a new sun to guide us, a holy book, tracked in new blood.

II

I load my own shells and have a suitcase of pressed
cardboard. Naturally I'm poor and picturesque.

My father is dead and doesn't care if his vault leaks,
that his casket is cheap, his son a poet and a liar.

All the honest farmers in my family's past are watching
me through the barn slats, from the corncrib and hogpen.

Ghosts demand more than wives & teachers. I'll make a
"V" of my two books and plow a furrow in the garden.

And I want to judge the poetry table at the County Fair.
A new form, poems stacked in pyramids like prize potatoes.

This county agent of poetry will tell poets, "More potash
& nitrogen, the rows are crooked and the field limp, depleted."

III

The alfalfa was sweet and damp in fields where shepherds
lay once and rams strutted and Indians left signs of war.

He harnesses the horses drawing the wagon of wheat toward
the road, ground froze, an inch of sifting snow around their feet.

She forks the hay into the mow, in winter is a hired girl
in town and is always tired when she gets up for school.

Asleep again between peach rows, drunk at midmorning and something
conclusive is needed, a tooth pulled, a fistfight, a girl.

Would any god come down from where and end a small war between
two walls of bone, brain veering, bucking in fatal velocity?

X

Praise me at Durkheim Fair where I've never been, hurling
grenade wursts at those who killed my uncle back in 1944.

Nothing is forgiven. The hurt child is thirty-one years old
and the girl in the pale blue dress walks out with another.

Where love lies. In the crawl space under the back porch
thinking of the aunt seen shedding her black bathing suit.

That girl was rended by the rapist. I'll send her a healing
sonnet in heaven. Forgive us. Forgive us. Forgive us.

The moon I saw through her legs beneath the cherry tree had
no footprints on it and a thigh easily blocked out its light.

Lauren Hutton has replaced Norma Jean, Ava Gardner, Lee Remick
and Vanessa Redgrave in my Calvinist fantasies. Don't go away.

XI

The brain opens the hand which touches that spot, clinically
soft, a member raises from his chair and insists upon his rights.

In some eye bank a cornea is frozen in liquid nitrogen. One day
my love I'll see your body from the left side of my face.

Half the team, a Belgian mare, was huge though weak. She died
convulsively from the 80-volt prod, still harnessed to her mate.

Alvin C. shot the last wolf in the Judith Basin after a four-year
hunt, raising a new breed of hounds to help. Dressed out 90 lbs.

When it rains I want to go north into the taiga, and before I
freeze in arid cold watch the reindeer watch the northern lights.

XXIII

I imagined her dead, killed by some local maniac who
crept upon the house with snowmobile at low throttle.

Alcohol that lets me play out hates and loves and fights;
in each bottle is a woman, the betrayer and the slain.

I insist on a one-to-one relationship with nature.
If Thursday I'm a frog it will have to be my business.

You are well. You grow taller. Friends think I've bought you
stilts but it is I shrinking, up past my knees in marl.

She said take out the garbage. I trot through a field with the
sack in my teeth. At the dump I pause to snarl at a rat.

XXIV

This amber light floating strangely upward in the woods—nearly
dark now with a warlock hooting through the tips of trees.

If I were to be murdered here as an Enemy of the State you would
have to bury me under that woodpile for want of a shovel.

She was near the window and beyond her breasts I could see
the burdock, nettles, goldenrod in a field beyond the orchard.

We'll have to abandon this place and live out of the car again.
You'll nurse the baby while we're stuck in the snow out of gas.

The ice had entered the wood. It was twenty below and the beech
easy to split. I lived in a lean-to covered with deerskins.

I have been emptied of poison and returned home dried
out with a dirty bill of health and screaming for new wine.

XXV

O happy day! Said *overpowered,* had by it all and transfixed
and unforgetting other times that refused to swirl and flow.

The calendar above my head made of unnatural numbers, day
lasted five days and I expect a splendid year's worth of dawn.

Rain pumps. Juliet in her tower and Gaspara Stampa again and
that girl lolling in the hammock with a fruit smell about her.

Under tag alder, beneath the ferns, crawling to know animals
for hours, how it looks to them down in this lightless place.

The girl out in the snows in the Laurentians saves her money
for Montreal and I am to meet her in a few years by "accident."

Magdalen comes in a waking dream and refuses to cover me,
crying out for ice, release from time, for a cool spring.

XXVI

What will I do with seven billion cubic feet of clouds
in my head? I want to be wise and dispense it for quarters.

All these push-ups are making me a muscular fatman. Love would
make me lean and burning. Love. Sorry the elevator's full.

She was zeroed in on by creeps and forgot my meaningful glances
from the door. But then I'm walleyed and wear used capes.

She was built entirely of makeup, greasepaint all the way through
like a billiard ball is a billiard ball beneath its hard skin.

We'll have to leave this place in favor of where the sun
is cold when seen at all, bones rust, it rains all day.

The cat is mine and so is the dog. You take the orchard,
house and car and parents. I'm going to Greenland at dawn.

XXXVI

A scenario: I'm the Star, Lauren, Faye, Ali, little stars,
we tour America in a '59 Dodge, they read my smoldering poems.

I climbed the chute and lowered myself onto the Brahma bull,
we jump the fence trampling crowds, ford rivers, are happy.

All fantasies of a life of love and laughter where I hold your
hand and watch suffering take the very first boat out of port.

The child lost his only quarter at the fair but under the grandstand
he finds a tunnel where all cowshit goes when it dies.

His epitaph: he could dive to the bottom or he paddled in black
water or bruised by flotsam he drowned in his own watery sign.

In the morning the sky was red as were his eyes and his brain
and he rolled over in the grass soaked with dew and said no.

LII

I was lucky enough to have invented a liquid heart
by drinking a full gallon of DNA stolen from a lab.

To discover eleven more dollars than you thought you
had and the wild freedom in the tavern that follows.

He's writing mood music for the dead again and ought to have
his ass kicked though it is bruised too much already by his sport.

Both serpent becoming dragon and the twelve moons lost
at sea, worshiped items, rifts no longer needed by us.

Hot Mickey Mouse jazz and the mice jigging up the path
to the beehive castle, all with the bleached faces of congressmen.

LV

The child crawls in widening circles, backs to the wall
as a dog would. The lights grow dim, his mother talks.

Swag: a hot night and the clouds running low were brains and I
above them with the moon saw down through a glass skull.

And O god I think I want to sleep within some tree
or on a warmer planet beneath a march of asteroids.

He saw the lady in the Empire dress raise it to sit bare
along the black tree branch where she sang a ditty of nature.

They are packing up in the lamplight, moving out again
for the West this time sure only of inevitable miracles.

No mail delights me as much as this—written with plum juice
on red paper and announcing the rebirth of three dead species.

LVI

God I am cold and want to go to sleep for a long time
and only wake up when the sun shines and dogs laugh.

I passed away in my sleep from general grief and a seven-
year hangover. Fat angels wrapped me in traditional mauve.

A local indian maiden of sixteen told the judge to go
fuck himself, got thirty days, died of appendicitis in jail.

I molded all the hashish to look like deer & rabbit turds
and spread them in the woods for rest stops when I walk.

Please consider the case closed. Otis Redding died in a
firestorm and we want to put him together again somehow.

LIX

On the fourteenth Sunday after Pentecost I rose early
and went fishing where I saw an osprey eat a bass in a tree.

We are not all guilty for anything. Let all stupefied
Calvinists take pleasure in sweet dirty pictures and gin.

As an active farmer I'm concerned. Apollinaire fertilizer
won't feed the pigs or chickens. Year of my seventh failure.

When we awoke the music was faint and a golden light came
through the window, one fly buzzed, she whispered another's name.

Let me announce I'm not against homosexuality. Now that the air
is clear on this issue you can talk freely Donny Darkeyes.

A home with a heated garage where dad can tinker with his
poetry on a workbench and mom glazes the steamed froth for lunch.

LXII

He climbed the ladder looking over the wall at the party
given for poets by the Prince of China. Fun was had by all.

A certain gracelessness entered his walk and gestures. A tumor
the size of a chickpea grew into a pink balloon in his brain.

I won't die in Paris or Jerusalem as planned but by electrocution
when I climb up the windmill to unscrew the shorted yard lights.

Samadhi. When I slept in the woods I awoke before dawn
and drank brandy and listened to the birds until the moon disappeared.

When she married she turned from a beautiful girl into a
useless sow with mud on her breasts and choruses of oinks.

O the bard is sure he loves the moon. And the inanimate moon
loves him back with silences, and moonbeams made of chalk.

LXV

There was a peculiar faint light from low in the east
and a leaf skein that scattered it on the ground where I lay.

I fell into the hidden mine shaft in Keewanaw, emerging
in a year with teeth and eyes of burnished copper, black skin.

What will become of her, what will become of her now that
she's sold into slavery to an Air Force lieutenant?

I spent the night prophesying to the huge black rock
in the river around which the current boiled and slid.

We'll have to put a stop to this dying everywhere of young
men. It's not working out and they won't come back.

Those poems you wrote won't raise the dead or stir the
living or open the young girl's lips to jubilance.

Letters to Yesenin

| 1973

I

to D.G.

This matted and glossy photo of Yesenin
bought at a Leningrad newsstand — permanently
tilted on my desk: he doesn't stare at me
he stares at nothing; the difference between
a plane crash and a noose adds up to nothing.
And what can I do with heroes with my brain fixed
on so few of them? Again nothing. Regard his flat
magazine eyes with my half-cocked own, both
of us seeing nothing. In the vodka was nothing
and Isadora was nothing, the pistol waved
in New York was nothing, and that plank bridge
near your village home in Ryazan covered seven feet
of nothing, the clumsy noose that swung the tilted
body was nothing but a noose, a law of gravity
this seeking for the ground, a few feet of nothing
between shoes and the floor a light-year away.
So this is a song of Yesenin's noose that came
to nothing, but did a good job as we say back home
where there's nothing but snow. But I stood under
your balcony in St. Petersburg, yes St. Petersburg!
a crazed tourist with so much nothing in my heart
it wanted to implode. And I walked down to the Neva
embankment with a fine sleet falling and there was
finally something, a great river vastly flowing, flat
as your eyes; something to marry to my nothing heart
other than the poems you hurled into nothing those
years before the articulate noose.

2

to Rose

I don't have any medals. I feel their lack
of weight on my chest. Years ago I was ambitious.
But now it is clear that nothing will happen.
All those poems that made me soar along a foot
from the ground are not so much forgotten as never
read in the first place. They rolled like moons
of light into a puddle and were drowned. Not even
the puddle can be located now. Yet I am encouraged
by the way you hanged yourself, telling me that such
things don't matter. You, the fabulous poet of
Mother Russia. But still, even now, schoolgirls
hold your dead heart, your poems, in their laps
on hot August afternoons by the river while they wait
for their boyfriends to get out of work or their
lovers to return from the army, their dead pets to
return to life again. To be called to supper. You
have a new life on their laps and can scent their
lavender scent, the cloud of hair that falls
over you, feel their feet trailing in the river,
or hidden in a purse walk the Neva again. Best of all
you are used badly like a bouquet of flowers to make
them shed their dresses in apartments. See those
steam pipes running along the ceiling. The rope.

3

I wanted to feel exalted so I picked up
Doctor Zhivago again. But the newspaper was there
with the horrors of the Olympics, those dead and
perpetually martyred sons of David. I want to present
all Israelis with .357 magnums so that they are
never to be martyred again. I wanted to be exalted
so I picked up *Doctor Zhivago* again but the TV was on
with a movie about the sufferings of convicts in
the early history of Australia. But then the movie
was over and the level of the bourbon bottle was dropping
and I still wanted to be exalted lying there with
the book on my chest. I recalled Moscow but I could
not place dear Yuri, only you Yesenin, seeing the Kremlin
glitter and ripple like Asia. And when drunk you appeared
as some Bakst stage drawing, a slain Tartar. But that is
all ballet. And what a dance you had kicking your legs from
the rope — We all change our minds, Berryman said in Minnesota
halfway down the river. Villon said of the rope that my neck
will feel the weight of my ass. But I wanted to feel exalted
again and read the poems at the end of *Doctor Zhivago* and
just barely made it. Suicide. Beauty takes my courage
away this cold autumn evening. My year-old daughter's red
robe hangs from the doorknob shouting *Stop*.

5

Lustra. Officially the cold comes from Manitoba;
yesterday at sixty knots. So that the waves mounted
the breakwater. The first snow. The farmers and carpenters
in the tavern with red, windburned faces. I am in there
playing the pinball machine watching all those delicious
lights flutter, the bells ring. I am halfway through
a bottle of vodka and am happy to hear Manitoba
howling outside. Home for dinner I ask my baby daughter
if she loves me but she is too young to talk. She cares
most about eating as I care most about drinking. Our wants
are simple as they say. Still when I wake from my nap
the universe is dissolved in grief again. The baby is sleeping
and I have no one to talk my language. My breath is shallow
and my temples pound. Vodka. Last October in Moscow I taught
a group of East Germans to sing "Fuck Nixon," and we were
quite happy until the bar closed. At the newsstand I saw a
picture of Bella Akhmadulina and wept. Vodka. You would have
liked her verses. The doorman drew near, alarmed. Outside
the KGB floated through the snow like arctic bats.
Maybe I belong there. They won't let me print my verses. On the
night train to Leningrad I will confess everything to someone.
All my books are remaindered and out of print. My face in
the mirror asks me who I am and says I don't know. But stop
this whining. I am alive and a hundred thousand acres of birches
around my house wave in the wind. They are women standing
on their heads. Their leaves on the ground today are small
saucers of snow from which I drink with endless thirst.

8

I cleaned the granary dust off your photo with my shirtsleeve.
Now that we are tidy we can wait for the host to descend
presumably from the sky as that seems to exhaust the alternatives.
You had a nice summer in the granary. I was out there with you
every day in June and July writing one of my six-week wonders,
another novel. Loud country music on the phonograph, wasps
and bees and birds and mice. The horses looked in the window
every hour or so, curious and rather stupid. Chief Joseph stared
down from the wall at both of us, a far nobler man than
we ever thought possible. We can't lead ourselves and he led
a thousand with a thousand horses a thousand miles. He was a god
and had three wives when one is usually more than enough for
a human. These past weeks I have been organizing myself into
my separate pieces. I have the limberness of a man twice my age
and this is as good a time as any to turn around. Joseph was
very understanding, incidentally, when the cavalry shot so many
of the women and children. It was to be expected. Earth is
full of precedents. They hang around like underground trees
waiting for their chance. The fish swam around four years solid
in preparation for August the seventh, 1972, when I took his life
and ate his body. Just as we may see our own ghosts next to
us whose shapes we will someday flesh out. All of this suffering
to become a ghost. Yours held a rope, manila, straight from
the tropics. But we don't reduce such glories to a mudbath.
The ghost giggles at genuflections. You can't buy him a drink.
Out in a clearing in the woods the other day I got up on a
stump and did a little dance for mine. We know the most fright-
ening time is noon. The evidence says I'm halfway there, such
wealth I can't give away, thirty-four years of seconds.

16

Today we've moved back to the granary again and I've anointed
the room with *Petrouchka*. Your story, I think. And music. That
ends with you floating far above in St. Petersburg's blue winter
air, shaking your fist among the fish and green horses, the dim-
inutive yellow sun and chicken playing the bass drum. Your
sawdust is spilled and you are forever borne by air. A simple story.
Another madman, Nijinsky, danced your part and you danced his.
None of us apparently is unique. Think of dying waving a fist full
of ballpoint pens that change into small snakes and that your
skull will be transposed into the cymbal it was always meant to be.
But shall we come down to earth? For years I have been too ready
to come down to earth. A good poet is only a sorcerer bored with
magic who has turned his attention elsewhere. O let us see wonders
that psilocybin never conceived of in her powdery head. Just now
I stepped on a leaf that blew in the door. There was a buzzing
and I thought it concealed a wasp, but the dead wasp turned out to be
a tiny bird, smaller than a hummingbird or june bug. Probably one
of a kind and I can tell no one because it would anger the swarm
of naturalists so vocal these days. I'll tuck the body in my hair
where it will remain forever a secret or tape it to the back of
your picture to give you more depth than any mirror on earth.
And another oddity: the record needle stuck just at the point
the trumpet blast announced the appearance of your ghost in the
form of Petrouchka. I will let it repeat itself a thousand times
through the afternoon until you stand beside the desk in your
costume. But I've no right to bring you back to life. We must
respect your affection for the rope. You knew the exact juncture
in your life when the act of dangling could be made a dance.

20

The mushrooms helped again: walking hangdoggedly to the granary
after the empty mailbox trip I saw across the barnyard at the base
of an elm stump a hundred feet away a group of white morels. How
many there were will be kept concealed for obvious reasons. While
I plucked them I considered each a letter from the outside world
to my little cul-de-sac, this valley: catching myself in this act
doing what I most despise, throwing myself in the laps of others.
Save my life. Help me. By return post. That sort of thing. So we
throw ourselves in the laps of others until certain famous laps
grow tired, vigorous laps whose movement is slowed by the freight
of all those cries. Then if you become famous after getting off
so many laps you can look at the beautiful women at your feet and
say I'll take that foot and that breast and that thigh and those lips
you have become so denatured and particular. They float and merge
their parts trying to come up with something that will please you.
Selecting the finest belly you write your name with a long thin
line of cocaine but she is perspiring and you can't properly snort
it off. Disappointments. The belly weeps but you dismiss her, sad
and frightened that your dreams have come to no end. Why cast Robert
Redford in your life story if all that he's going to do is sit there
and piss and moan at the typewriter for two hours in expensive
Eastman color? Not much will happen if you don't like to drink
champagne out of shoes. And sated with a half-dozen French meals a day
you long for those simple boiled potatoes your estranged wife made
so perfectly. The letters from your children are defiled in a stack
of fan mail and obscene photos. Your old dog and horse have been
given to kindly people and your wife will soon marry a jolly farmer.
No matter that your million-selling books are cast in bronze. On a
whim you fly to Palm Beach, jump on your yacht and set the automatic.
You fit a nylon hawser around your neck, hurl overboard, and after
the sharks have lunch your head skips in the noose like a marlin bait.

21

To answer some of the questions you might ask were you alive and
had we become friends but what do poets ask one another after long
absence? How have you been other than dead and how have I been
dying on earth without naming the average string of complaints which
is only worrying aloud, naming the dreaded motes that float around
the brain, those pink balloons calling themselves poverty, failure,
sickness, lust, and envy. To mention a very few. But you want part-
iculars, not the human condition or a letter to the editor on why
when I'm at my worst I think I've been fucked over. So here's this
Spring's news: now that the grass is taller I walk in some fear of
snakes. Feeling melancholy I watched my wife plant the garden row
on row while the baby tried to catch frogs. It's hard not to eat too
much when you deeply love food but I've limited myself to a half
gallon of Burgundy a day. On long walks my eyes are so sunk back
in my brain they see nothing, then move forward again toward the light
and see a high meadow turning pale green and swimming in the fog
with crows tracing perceptible and geometrical paths just above
the fog but audible. At the shore I cast for fish, some of them
large with deliquescing smelt and alewives in their bellies. Other
than marriage I haven't been in love for years; close calls over
the world I mentioned to you before, but it's not love if it isn't
a surprise. I look at women and know deeply they are from another
planet and sometimes even lightly touching a girl's arm I know
I am touching a lovely though alien creature. We don't get back
those days we don't caress, don't make love. If I could get you out
in the backcountry down in Key West and get some psilocybin into
you you would cut your legendary vodka consumption. Naturally I
still believe in miracles and the holy fate of the imagination. How
is it being dead and would I like it and should I put it off for a while?

26

Going in the bar last Sunday night I noticed that they were having
high-school graduation down the street. Caps and gowns. June and
mayflies fresh from the channel fluttering in the warm still air.
After a few drinks I felt jealous and wanted someone to say, "Best of
luck in your chosen field," or, "The road of life is ahead of you."
Remember your first trip to Moscow at nineteen? Everything was pos-
sible. You watched those noblewomen at the riding academy who would
soon be permanently unhorsed, something you were to have mixed
feelings about, what with the way poets suck up to and are attracted
to the aristocracy however gimcrack. And though the great Blok
welcomed you, you felt tentative, an unknown quantity, and remained
so for several years. But how quickly one goes from being unknown
and embarrassed to bored and arrogant, from being ignored to expecting
deference. From fleabag rooms to at least the Plaza. And the daydreams
and hustling, the fantasies and endless work that get you from one
to the other, only to discover that you really want to go home. Start
over with a new deck. But back home all the animals are dead, the
friends have disappeared and the fields gone to weed. The fish
have flown from the creeks and ponds and the birds have all drowned
or gone to China. No one knows you—they have little time for poetry
in the country, or in the city for that matter except for the minis-
trations of a few friends. Your name bobs up like a Halloween
apple and literature people have the vague feeling that they should read
you if they ever "catch up" on their reading. Once on a train I saw
a girl reading a book of mine but she was homely and I had a toothache
so I let the moment pass. What delicious notoriety. The journalist
said I looked like a bricklayer or beer salesman, not being fashion-
ably slender. But lately the sun shines through, the sweet release
of flinging these lines at the dead, almost like my baby Anna throw-
ing grain to the horses a mile away, in the far corner of the pasture.

We're nearing the end of this homage that often resembles a
suicide note to a suicide. I didn't mean it that way but how
often our hands sneak up on our throats and catch us unaware.
What are you doing here we say. Don't squeeze so hard. The hands
inside the vodka bottle and on the accelerator, needles and coke-
sore noses. It's not very attractive, is it? But now there is rain
on the tin roof, the world outside is green and leafy with bluebirds
this morning dive-bombing drowning worms from a telephone wire,
the baby laughing as the dog eats the thirty-third snake of the
summer. And the bodies on the streets and beaches. Girl bottoms!
Holy. Tummies in the sun! Very probably holy. Peach evidence almost
struggling for air! A libidinal stew that calls us to life however
ancient and basal. May they plug their lovely ears with their big
toes. God surely loves them to make them look that way and can I
do less than He at least in this respect. As my humble country
father said in our first birds-and-bees talk so many years ago: "That
thing ain't just to pee through." This vulgarity saves us as
certainly as our chauvinism. Just now in midafternoon I wanted
a tumbler of wine but John Calvin said, "You got up at noon. No wine
until you get your work done. You haven't done your exercises to
suppress the gut the newspaper says women find most disgusting.
The fence isn't mended and the neighbor's cow keeps crawling through
in the night, stealing the fresh clover you are saving for Rachel
the mare when she drops her foal." So the wine bottle remains
corked and Calvin slips through the floorboards to the crawl space
where he spends all of his time hating his body. Would these concerns
have saved you? Two daughters and a wife. Children prop our rotting
bodies with cries of *earn earn earn*. On occasion we are kissed. So odd
in a single green month to go from the closest to so far from death.

30

The last and I'm shrinking from the coldness of your spirit: that
chill lurid air that surrounds great Lenin in his tomb as if we
had descended into a cloud to find on the catafalque a man who has
usurped nature, isn't dead any more than you or I are dead. Only
unlikely to meet and talk to our current forms. Today I couldn't
understand words so I scythed ragweed and goldenrod before it could
go to seed and multiply. I played with god imagining how to hold His
obvious scythe that caught you, so unlike the others, aware and
cooperative. Is He glad to help if we're willing? A boring question
since we're so able and ingenious. Sappho's sparrows are always
telling us that love will save us, some *other* will arrive to draw
us cool water, lie down with us in our private darkness and make
us well. I think not. What a fabulous lie. We've disposed of sparrows
and god, the death of color, those who are dominated by noon and
the vision of night flowing in your ears and eyes and down your
throat. But we didn't mean to arrive at conclusions. Fifty years are
only a moment between this granary and a hanged man half the earth
away. You are ten years younger than my grandmother Hulda who still
sings Lutheran hymns and watches the Muskegon River flow. In whatever
we do, we do damage to ourselves; and in those first images there
were always cowboys or cossacks fighting at night, murdered animals
and girls never to be touched; dozing with head on your dog's chest
you understand breath and believe in golden cities where you will
live forever. And that fatal expectancy—not comprehending that we
like our poems are flowers for the void. In those last days you
wondered why they turned their faces. Any common soul knew you
had consented to death, the only possible blasphemy. I write to
you like some half-witted, less courageous brother, unwilling to tease
those ghosts you slept with faithfully until they cast you out.

At 8:12 a.m. all of the watches in the world are being wound.
Which is not quite the same thing as all of the guitars on earth
being tuned at midnight. Or that all suicides come after the mail-
man when all hope is gone. Before the mailman, watches are wound,
windows looked through, shoes precisely tied, tooth care, the
attenuations of the hangover noted. Which is not the same as
the new moon after midnight or her bare feet stepping slowly toward
you and the snake easing himself from the ground for a meal.
The world is so necessary. Someone must execute stray dogs and
free the space they're taking up. I can see people walking down
Nevsky Prospekt winding their watches before you were discovered
too far above the ground, that mystical space that was somewhere
occupied by a stray dog or a girl in an asylum on her hands
and knees. A hanged face turns slowly from a plum to a lump of
coal. I'm winding my watch in antipathy. I see the cat racing
around the yard in a fantasy of threat. She's preparing for
eventualities. She prizes the only prize. But we aren't the cats
we once were thousands of years ago. You didn't die with the
dignity of an animal. Today you make me want to tie myself to
a tree, stake my feet to earth herself so I can't get away. It didn't
come as a burning bush or pillar of light but I've decided to stay.

Returning to Earth

| 1977

RETURNING TO EARTH

She
pulls the sheet of this dance
across me
then runs, staking
the corners far out at sea.

—

So curious in the middle of America, the only "locus"
I know, to live and love at great distance. (Growing
up, everyone is willing to drive seventy miles to see
a really big grain elevator, ninety miles for a dance,
two hundred to look over a pair of Belgian mares
returning the next day for the purchase, three hundred
miles to see Hal Newhouser pitch in Detroit, eight
hundred miles to see the Grand Ole Opry, a thousand
miles to take the mongoloid kid to a Georgia faith healer.)
I hitched two thousand for my first glimpse of the Pacific.
When she first saw the Atlantic she said near Key Largo,
"I thought it would be bigger."

—

I widowed my small
collection of magic
until it poisoned itself with longing.
I have learned nothing.
I give orders to the rain.
I tried to catch the tempest in a gill net.
The stars seem a little closer lately.
I'm no longer afraid to die
but is this a guidepost of lunacy?
I intend to see the ten hundred million worlds Mañjushri

passed through before he failed to awaken the maiden.
Taking off and landing are the dangerous times.
I was commanded in a dream to dance.

—

O Faustus talks to himself,
talks to himself, talks to himself,
talks to himself, talks to himself,
Faustus talks to himself,
talks to himself.

—

Ikkyū's ten years near the whorehouses
shortens distances, is truly palpable;
and in ten years you will surely
get over your itch. Or not.

—

Don't waste yourself staring at the moon.
All of those moon-staring-rear-view-mirror deaths!
Study the shadow of the horse turd in the grass.
There must be a difference between looking at a picture
of a bird and the actual bird (barn swallow)
fifteen feet from my nose on the shed eaves.
That cloud SSW looks like the underside
of a river in the sky.

—

O I'm lucky
got a car that starts almost every day
tho' I want a new yellow Chevy pickup
got two letters today
and I'd rather have three
have a lovely wife

but want all the pretty ones
got three white hawks in the barn
but want a Himalayan eagle
have a planet in the basement
but would prefer the moon in the granary
have the northern lights
but want the Southern Cross.

—

The stillness of this earth
which we pass through
with the precise speed of our dreams.

—

I'm getting very old. If I were a mutt
in dog years I'd be seven, not stray so far.
I am large. Tarpon my age are often large
but they are inescapably fish. A porpoise
my age was the King of New Guinea in 1343.
Perhaps I am the king of my dogs, cats, horses,
but I have dropped any notion of explaining
to them why I read so much. To be mysterious
is a prerogative of kingship. I discovered
lately that my subjects do not live a life,
but are life itself. They do not recognize
the pain of the schizophrenia of kingship.
To them I am pretty much a fellow creature.

—

So distances: yearns for Guayaquil and Petersburg,
the obvious Paris and Rome,
restraint in the Cotswolds, perfumes of Arusha,
Entebbe bristling with machine guns,
also Ecuadorian & Ethiopian airports,

border guards always whistling in boredom
and playing with machine guns;
all to count the flies on the lion's eyelids
and the lioness hobbling in deep grass
lacking one paw, to scan the marlin's caudal fin
cutting the Humboldt swell, an impossible scissors.

—

There must be a cricket named Zagreus
in the granary tucked under a roof beam,
under which my three-year-old daughter
boogies madly,
her first taste of the Grateful Dead;
she is well out of her mind.

—

Rain on the tin roof which covers a temple,
rain on my walking head which covers a temple,
rain covering my laugh shooting
toward the woods for no reason,
rain splattering in pasture's heat
raising cones of dust,
and off the horses' backs,
on oriole's nest in ash tree,
on my feet poking out the door,
testing the endurance of our actual pains,
biting hard against the sore tooth.

—

She's rolling in the bear fat
She's rolling in the sand
She's climbing a vine
She's boarding a jet
She flies into the distance wearing blue shoes

Having become the person I most feared in Childhood –
A DRUNKARD. They were pointed out to us
in our small town: oil workers, some poor farmers
(on Saturday marketing), a mechanic, a fired teacher.
They'd stumble when walking, sometimes yell
on the street at noon, wreck their old cars;
their wives would request special prayers in church,
and the children often came to school in winter
with no socks. We took up a collection to buy
the dump-picker's daughter shoes. Also my uncles
are prone to booze, also my father though it was well-
controlled, and now my fifteen-year war with the bottle
with whiskey removing me from the present
in a sweet, laughing haze, removing anger, anxiety,
instilling soft grandness, decorating ugliness
and reaffirming my questionable worth. SEE: Olson's
fingers touch his thumb, encircling the bottle—he
gulps deeply, talking through one night into the next
afternoon, talking, basking in Gorton's fishy odor.
So many of my brethren seem to die of busted guts.
Now there is a measured truce with maps and lines
drawn elegantly against the binge, concessions,
measurings, hesitant steps. My favorite two bars
are just north and barely south of the 45th parallel.

—

I no longer believe in the idea of magic,
christs, the self, metal buddhas, bibles.
A horse is only the space his horseness requires.
If I pissed in the woods would a tree see my ear
fall off and would the ear return to the body
on the morning of the third day? Do bo trees

ever remember the buddhas who've slept beneath them?
I admit that yesterday I built an exploratory altar.
Who can squash his delight in incomprehension?
So on a piece of old newspaper I put an earthworm
on a maple leaf, the remains of a bluebird after
the cat was finished—head and feet, some dog hair,
shavings from when we trimmed the horses' hooves,
a snakeskin, a stalk of ragweed, a gourd,
a lemon, a cedar splinter, a nonsymbolic doorknob,
a bumblebee with his juice sucked out by a wasp.
Before this altar I invented a doggerel mantra
it is this   it is this   it is this

—

It is very hard to give birds advice.
They are already members of eternity.
In their genes they have both compass
and calendar. Their wing bones are hollow.
We are surprised by how light a dead bird is.

—

But what am I penetrating?
Only that it seems nothing convinces
itself or anyone else reliably
of its presence. It is in the distance.

—

No Persephone in my life,
Ariadne, Helen, Pocahontas,
Evangeline of the Book House
but others not less extraordinary who step
lightly into the dream life, refusing to leave:
girl in a green dress,
woman lolling in foot-deep Caribbean,

woman on balcony near Vatican,
girl floating across Copley Square in 1958,
mythologized woman in hut in 1951,
girl weeping in lilacs,
woman slapping my face,
girl smoking joint in bathtub looking at big toe,
slender woman eating three lobsters,
woman who blew out her heart with cocaine,
girl livid and deformed in dreams,
girl breaking the window in rage,
woman sick in hotel room,
heartless woman in photo –
not heartless but a photo.

—

My left eye is nearly blind.
No words have ever been read with it.
Not that the eye is virgin—thirty years ago
it was punctured by glass. In everything
it sees a pastel mist. The poster of Chief Joseph
could be King Kong, Hong Kong, a naked lady riding
a donkey into Salina, Kansas. A war atrocity.
This eye is the perfect art critic. This eye
is a perfect lover saying bodies don't matter,
it is the voice. This eye can make a lightbulb
into the moon when it chooses. Once a year I open
it to the full moon out in the pasture and yell,
white light white light.

—

A half-dozen times a day
I climb through the electric fence
on my way and back to my study
in the barnyard. I have to be cautious.

I have learned my true dimensions,
how far my body sticks out from my brain.

—

We are each
the only world
we are going to get.

—

I don't want to die. It would certainly
inconvenience my wife and daughters.
I am sufficiently young that it would help
my publisher unpack his warehouse of books.
It would help me stop drinking and lose weight.
I could talk to Boris Pasternak.
He never saw the film.

—

Wanting to pull the particular nail
that will collapse the entire house
so that there is nothing there,
not even a foundation: a rubble heap,
no sign at all, just grass, weeds and trees
among which you cannot find a shard of masonry,
which like an arrowhead might suggest
an entire civilization.

—

She was lying back in the rowboat.
It was hot.
She tickled me with her toes.
She picked lily pads.
She watched mating dragonflies.
"How many fish below us?"

"O a hundred or so."
"It would be fun to fall in love with someone."
The rower continued his rowing.

—

Why be afraid of a process you're
already able to describe with precision?
To say you don't believe in it
is to say that you're *not*.
It doesn't care so why should you?
You've been given your body back
without a quarrel. See this vision
of your imagined body float toward you:
it disappears into you without a trace.
You feel full with a fullness again.
Your dimensions aren't scattered in dreams.

—

This fat pet bird I've kept so many years,
a crow with a malformed wing
tucked against its side, no doubt a vestigial fin:
I taught him early to drink from my whiskey
or wineglass in the shed but he prefers wine.
He flies only in circles of course
but when he drinks he flies in great
circles miles wide, preferring bad days
with low cold clouds looking like leper brains.
I barely hear his whimps & howls: O jesus
the pain O shit it hurts O god let it end.
He drags himself through air mostly landing
near a screen door slamming, a baby's cry,
a dog's bark, a forest fire, a sleeping coyote.
These fabulous memories of earth!

—

Not to live in fancy
these short hours: let shadows
fall from walls as shadows, nothing else.
New York is exactly
dead center
in New York.
Not to indulge this heartsickness as failure.
Did I write three songs or seven
or half-a-one, one line, phrases?
A single word
that might hang in the still, black air
for more than a few moments?
Then the laughter comes again.
We sing it away.
What short wicks
we fuel with our blood.

—

Disease!
My prostate beating & pulsing
down there like a frightened turkey's heart.

—

A cold day,
low ceiling.
A cloud the size
of a Greyhound bus
just hit the house.

—

Offenses this summer against Nature:
poured iced tea on a garter snake's head

as he or she dozed on the elm stump,
pissed on a bumblebee (inattentive),
kicked a thousand wasps to death in my slippers.
Favors done this summer for Nature:
let the mice keep their nest in the green station wagon,
let Rachel the mare breathe her hot damp horse breath
against my bare knee when she wanted to,
tried without success to get the song sparrow out
of the shed where she had trapped herself fluttering
along the cranny under the assumption that the way *out*
is always the way *up,* and her wings lie to her
with each separate beat against the ceiling saying
there is no way down and out,
there is no way down and out,
the open door back into the world.

—

Coleridge's pet spider
he says is very intellectual,
spins webs of deceit
straight out of his big
hanging ass.

—

Mandrill, *Mandrillus sphinx,*
crest, mane, beard, yellow, purple, green,
a large fierce, gregarious baboon —
has small wit but ties himself to a typewriter
with wolfish and bloody appetite.
He is just one, thousands will follow,
something true to be found among the countless
millions of typed pages. There's a picture
of him in Tibet though no mandrills have been known
to live there. He wants to be with his picture

though there's no way to get there. So he types.
So he dreams *lupanar lupanar lupanar*
brothels with steam and white dust, music
that describes undiscovered constellations
so precisely the astronomers of the next century
will know where to look. Peaches dripping light.
Lupanar. The female arriving in dreams is unique,
not another like her on earth; she's created for a moment.
It only happens one time. One time O one time.
He types. She's his only real food.
O *lupanar* of dreams.

—

Head bobbing right and left,
with no effort
and for the first time
I see all sides of the pillar at once,
the earth,   her body.

—

I can't jump
high anymore.

—

He tightens
pumps in blue cold air
gasoline
the electricity from summer storms
the seven-by-seven-foot
blue face of lightning
that shot down the gravel road
like a ghost rocket.

—

Saw the lord of crows
late at night in my living room;
don't know what true color of man –
black-white-red-yellow –
as he was hooded with the mask of a crow;
arms, legs, with primary feathers sewn to leather
downy black breast
silver bells at wrist
long feathered tail
dancing for a moment or two then disappearing.
Only in the morning did it occur to me
that it was a woman.

—

What sways us is not each other
but our dumb insistent pulse beating
I was I am I will I was
sometimes operatic, then in church
or barroom tenor, drunkenly, in prayer,
slowly in the confusion of dreams
but the same tripartite, the three
of being here trailing off into itself,
no finale any more than a beginning
until all of us lie buried
in the stupefying ache of caskets.

—

This earth of intentions.
Moonfucked, you can't eat or drink
or sleep at ten feet. Kneeling, love
is at nose tip. Or wound about
each other our eyes forget that they are eyes
and begin to see. You remember individual
fence posts, fish, trees, ankles,

from your tenth year.
Those savages lacking other immediate alternatives
screwed the ground to exhaustion.

—

Bad art: walking away untouched, unmoving,
barely tickled, *amused,* diverted killing time,
throwing salt on the grass. The grace of Yukio Mishima's
suicide intervening in the false harmony,
Kawabata decides to live longer, also a harmony.
In bad music, the cheapest and easiest way to get
out of it infers Clapton. Eros girdled in metal
and ozone. A man in a vacuum of images, stirring
his skull with his dick, sparing himself his future,
fancy bound, unparticular, unpeculiar, following
the strings of his dreaming to more dreaming
in a sump narcosis, never having given himself
over to his life, never owning an instant.

—

Week's eating log:
whitefish poached with lemon, onion, wine, garlic;
Chulapa—pork roasted twelve hours with pinto beans,
red peppers, chili powder; grilled twenty-two pounds
of beef ribs for friends; a lamb leg pasted with Dijon
mustard, soy, garlic; Chinese pork ribs; *menudo*
just for Benny & me as no one else would eat it –
had to cook tripe five hours then mix with hominy
and peppers with chorizo tacos on the side;
copious fresh vegetables, Burgundy, Colombard, booze
with all of the above; at night fevered dreams
of her sumptuous butt, a Mercator projection,
the map of an enormous meal in my brain.
Still trying to lose weight.

—

How strange to see a horse
stare
straight up.

—

Everything is a good idea at the time.
Staring with stupid longing at a picture, dumbstruck
as they used to call it, an instant's whimsy;
a body needlessly unlike any other's,
deserved by someone so monstrous
as Lucrezia Borgia: how do you come to terms
with it? thinks the American. You don't, *terms*
being a financial word not applicable
to bodies. Wisdom shies away, the packhorse
startled at the diamondback beneath the mesquite,
the beauty of threat. Now look at her as surely
as that other beast, the dead crow beneath the apple
tree so beautiful in its black glossiness
but without eyes, feet stiff and cool as the air.
I watched it for a year and owned its bleached
shinbone but gave it to someone who needed
the shinbone of a crow.

—

She says it's too hot,
the night's too short,
that I'm too drunk,
but it's not *too* anything, ever.

—

Living all my life with a totally normal-sized dick
(cf. the authorities: Van de Velde, Masters & Johnson)
neither hedgehog or horse, neither emu or elephant

(saw one in Kenya, the girls said O my goodness)
neither wharf rat, arrogant buck dinosaur,
prepotent swan, ground squirrel, Lauxmont Admiral
famous Holstein bull who sired 200,000 artificially.
I am saved from trying to punish anyone,
from confusing it with a gun, harpoon, cannon, sword,
cudgel, Louisville Slugger. It just sits there
in the dark, shy and friendly
like the new kid at school.

—

In our poetry we want to rub our nose hard
into whatever is before it; to purge
these dreams of pictures, photos, phantom people.
She offers a flex of butt, belly button, breasts,
slight puff of veneris, gap in teeth often capped,
grace of knees, high cheekbones and neck,
all the thickness of paper. The grandest illusion
as in ten thousand movies in all those hours
of dark, the only true sound the exploding
popcorn and the dairy fetor of butter. After the movie
a stack of magazines at the drugstore
to filter through, to be filtered through.

—

A choral piece for a dead dog:
how real the orchestra and hundred
voices on my lawn; pagan with the dog
on a high cedar platform to give the fire
its full marriage of air; the chorus
sings DOG a thousand times, dancing
in a circle. That would be a proper
dog funeral. By god. No dreams here
but a mighty shouting of *dog*.

—

Sunday night,
I'm lucky to have all of this vodka,
a gift of Stolichnaya.
And books. And a radio
playing WSM all the way from Nashville.
Four new pups in the bedroom.
The house snores. My tooth aches.
It is time to fry an egg.

—

Heard the foghorn out at sea,
saw horses' backs shiny with rain,
felt my belly jiggle as I walked
through the barnyard in a light rain
with my daughter's small red umbrella
to protect the not-very-precious manuscript,
tiptoeing barefoot in the tall wet grass
trying to avoid the snakes.

—

With all this rain
the pond is full.
The ducks are one week old
and already speak their language perfectly –
a soft nasal hiss.
With no instructions they skim bugs from the pond's
surface and look fearfully at me.

—

The minister whacks off as does the insurance man,
habitual golfer, sweet lady in her bower,
as do novelists, monks, nuns in nunneries,
maidens in dormitories, stallion against fence post,

goat against puzzled pig who does not cease feeding,
and so do senators, generals, wives during TV
game shows, movie stars and football players, students
to utter distraction, teachers, butchers, world leaders,
everyone except poets who fear the dreaded
growth of hair on the palms, blindness.
They know that even in an empty hotel room
in South Dakota that someone is watching.

—

With my dog
I watched a single crow
fly across the field.
We are each one.

—

Thirty feet up in the air
near the top of my novel I want a bird to sing
from the crown of the barn roof.
A hundred feet away there is a grove of trees,
maple and elm and ash,
placed quite accidentally before any of us were born.
Everyone remembers who planted the lilacs
forty years and three wars ago.

—

In the morning paper
the arsonist
who was also a paranoid schizophrenic,
a homosexual,
retarded,
an alcoholic
who lacerated his body with a penknife
and most significantly for the rest of us,

started fires where none were desired,
on whim.

—

Spent months regathering dreams lost in the diaspora,
all of the prism's colors, birds, animals, bodies,
getting them back within the skin
where they'd do no damage.
How difficult catching them armed
only with a butterfly-catcher's net,
a gun, airplane, an ice pick,
a chalice of rainwater, a green headless
buddha on loan from a veteran of foreign wars.

—

Saw that third eye in a dream
but couldn't remember if it looked
from a hole in a wall of ice,
or a hole in a floor of ice,
but it was an eye looking from a hole in ice.

—

Two white-faced cattle out in the dark-green pasture,
one in the shade of the woodlot,
one out in the hot sunlight,
eating slowly and staring at each other.

—

So exhausted after my walk from orchestrating
the moves of one billion August grasshoppers
plus fifty thousand butterflies
swimming at the heads
of fifty thousand wildflowers
red blue yellow orange

orange flowers the only things that rhyme with orange
the one rabbit in the pasture
one fly buzzing at the window
a single hot wind through the window
a man sitting at my desk resembling me.

—

He sneaks up on the temple slowly at noon.
He's so slow it seems like it's taking years.
Now his hands are on a pillar, the fingers
encircling it, with only the tips inside the gate.

—

After all of this long moist dreaming
I perceive how accurate the rooster's crow
is from down the road.

—

You can suffer and not even know you're suffering
because you've been suffering so long you can't remember
another life. You're actually a dead dog on a country road.
And a man gets used to his rotten foot.
After a while it's simply a rotten foot,
and his rotten ideas are even easier to get used to
because they don't hurt as much as a rotten foot.
The road from Belsen to Watergate paved
with perfectly comfortable ideas, ideas to sleep on
like a mattress stuffed with money and death,
an actual waterbed filled with liquid gold.
So our inept tuna cravings and Japan's (she imitates
our foulest features) cost an annual
250,000 particular dolphin deaths,
certainly as dear as people to themselves
or so the evidence says.

—

Near my lover's old frame house with a field
behind it, the grass is a brilliant gold.
Standing on the gravel road before the house
a great flock of blackbirds coming over so close
to my head I see them all individually,
eyes, crests, the feet drawn out in flight.

—

I owe the dentist nine hundred dollars.
This is more than I made on three
of my books of poems. But then I am gloriously
free. I can let my mouth rot and quit
writing poems. I could let the dentist
write the poems while I walked into the dark
with a tray of golden teeth I'd sculpt
for myself in the forms of shark's teeth,
lion's teeth, teeth of grizzly and python.
Watch me open my mouth as I wear these wondrous
teeth. The audience gross is exactly nine hundred!
The house lights dim. My lips part.
There is a glimpse of sun.

—

Abel always votes.
Cain usually thinks better of it
knowing not very deep in his heart
that no one deserves to be encouraged.
Abel has a good job & is a responsible screw,
but many intelligent women seem drawn
to Crazy Horse, a descendant of Cain,
even if he only gets off his buffalo pony
once a year to throw stones at the moon.

Of course these women marry Abel but at bars and parties
they are the first to turn to the opening door
to see who is coming in.

—

I was standing near the mow door
in the darkness, a party going on in the château.
She was there with her sister.
We kissed then lay down on fresh straw in a paddock.
An angry stallion jumped over on top of us.
I could see his outline clearly against the sky.
Why did we die so long ago.

—

How wind, cloud and water
blaspheme symmetry at every instant,
forms that can't be remembered and stored:
Grand Marais, Cape Ann at Eastern Point,
Lake Manyara from a cliff, Boca Grande's sharks
giving still water a moving shape—they are there
and there and there—the waterfall next to a girl
so obviously on a white horse, to mud
puddle cat avoids, back to Halibut Point,
Manitou convulsed in storms to thousand-mile
weed line in Sargasso Sea to brown violent confluence
of Orinoco and ocean off Devil's Gate; mixing wind,
cloud, water, the purest mathematics of their
description studied as glyphs, alchemists
everywhere working with humble gold, somewhere to begin,
having to keep eyes closed to wind, cloud, water.

—

Saw an ox. A black horse I recognized.
A procession of carts full of flowers

pulled by nothing. Asymmetrical planets.
Fish out of their element of water.
Simple music—a single note an hour.
How are we to hear it, if at all?
No music in statement, the lowest denominator
by which our fragments can't find each other.
But I can still hear the notes of April,
the strained, fragile notes of March:
convalescent, tentative, a weak drink
taken over and over in immense doses.
It is the body that is the suite entire,
brain firmly fused to the trunk, spine
more actual than mountains, brain moving
as a river, governed precisely by her energies.

—

Whippoorwill. Mourning dove. Hot morning rain
changing to a violent squall coming SSW out of the lake,
thunder enveloping itself then unfolding
as cloth in wind furls, holds back, furls again;
running nearly naked in shorts to my shed,
thunder rattling windows and walls,
acorns rattling against barn's tin roof;
the floor shudders, then stillness as squall passes,
as strange as a strong wind at summer twilight
when the air is yellow. Now cool still air.
Mourning dove.
Oriole.

—

O my darling sister
O she crossed over
she's crossed over
is planted now near her father

six feet under earth's skin —
their still point on this whirling earth
now and I think forever.

—

Now it is as close to you as the clothes you wear.
The clothes are attached to your body
by a cord that runs up your spine, out your neck
and through the earth, back up your spine.

—

At nineteen I began to degenerate,
slight smell of death in my gestures,
unbelieving, tentative, wailing...
so nineteen years have gone. It doesn't matter.
It might have taken fifty. Or never.
Now the barriers are dissolving, the stone fences
in shambles. I want to have my life
in cloud shapes, water shapes, wind shapes,
crow call, marsh hawk swooping over grass and weed tips.
Let the scavenger take what he finds.
Let the predator love his prey.

Selected & New Poems

| 1982

FOLLOWERS

Driving east on Buddha's birthday,
April 9, 1978, past my own birthplace
Grayling, Michigan, south 300 miles to Toledo,
then east again to New York for no reason –
belled heart swinging in grief for months
until I wanted to take my life in my hands;
three crows from home followed above
the car until the Delaware River where
they turned back: one stood all black
and lordly on a fresh pheasant killed
by a car: all this time
counting the mind, counting crows,
each day's ingredients
the same, barring rare
bad luck
good luck
dumb luck
all set in marble by the habitual,
locked as the day passes moment by moment:
say on the tracks the train can't
turn 90 degrees to the right because it's not
the nature of a train,
but we think a man can dive
in a pond, swim across it,
and climb a tree though few of us do.

GATHERING APRIL

for Simic

Stuffing a crow call in one ear
and an unknown bird's in the other,
lying on the warm cellar door out of
the cool wind which I take small sparing
bites of with three toes still wet from the pond's
edge: April is so violent up here you hide
in corners or, when in the woods, in swales
and behind beech trees. Twenty years ago
this April I offered my stupid heart up to
this bloody voyage. It was near a marsh
on a long walk. You can't get rid of those
thousand pointless bottles of whiskey
that you brought along. Last night after
the poker game I read Obata's Li Po.
He was no less a fool but adding those
twenty thousand poems you come up
with a god. There are patents on all
the forms of cancer but still we praise
god from whom or which all blessings flow:
that an April exists, that a body lays itself
down on a warm cellar door and remembers, drinks
in birds and wind, whiskey, frog songs
from the marsh, the little dooms hiding
in the shadow of each fence post.

The Theory & Practice of Rivers
and New Poems

| 1989

THE THEORY & PRACTICE OF RIVERS

In memoriam
GLORIA ELLEN HARRISON
1964–1979

The rivers of my life:
moving looms of light,
anchored beneath the log
at night I can see the moon
up through the water
as shattered milk, the nudge
of fishes, belly and back
in turn grating against log
and bottom; and letting go, the current
lifts me up and out
into the dark, gathering motion,
drifting into an eddy
with a sideways swirl,
the sandbar cooler than the air:
to speak it clearly,
how the water goes
is how the earth is shaped.

It is not so much that I got
there from here, which is everyone's
story: but the shape
of the voyage, how it pushed
outward in every direction
until it stopped:
roots of plants and trees,
certain coral heads,
photos of splintered lightning,
blood vessels,
the shapes of creeks and rivers.

This is the ascent out of water:
there is no time but that
of convenience, time so that everything
won't happen at once; dark
doesn't fall—dark comes up
out of the earth, an exhalation.
It gathers itself close
to the ground, rising
to envelop us, as if the bottom
of the sea rose up to meet us.
Have you ever gone
to the bottom of the sea?

Mute unity of water.
I sculpted this girl
out of ice so beautifully
she was taken away.
How banal the swan song
which is a water song.
There never was a swan
who said good-bye. My raven
in the pine tree squawked his way
to death, falling from branch
to branch. To branch again.
To ground. The song, the muffle
of earth as the body falls,
feather against pine needles.

Near the estuary north of Guilford
my brother recites the Episcopalian
burial service over his dead daughter.
Gloria, as in *Gloria in Excelsis*.
I cannot bear this passion and courage;
my eyes turn toward the swamp

and sea, so blurred they'll never quite
clear themselves again. The inside of the eye,
vitreous humor, is the same pulp found
inside the squid. I can see Gloria
in the snow and in the water. She lives
in the snow and water and in my eyes.
This is a song for her.

Kokopele saved me this time:
flute song in soft dark
sound of water over rock,
the moon glitter rippling;
breath caught as my hunched
figure moved in a comic circle,
seven times around the cabin
through the woods in the dark.
Why did I decide to frighten myself?

Light snow in early May,
wolf prints in alluvial fan,
moving across the sandbar
in the river braided near its mouth
until the final twist; then the prints
move across drift ice in a dead
channel, and back into the swamp.

The closest I came to describing it:
it is early winter, mid-November
with light snow, the ground rock-hard
with frost. We are moving but I can't
seem to find my wife and two daughters.
I have left our old house and can't remember
how to find the new one.

The days are stacked against
what we think we are:
the story of the water babies
swimming up- and downstream
amid waterweed, twisting
with cherubic smiles in the current,
human and fish married.
Again! The girl I so painfully
sculpted out of ice
was taken away. She said:
"Goddamn the Lizard King,"
her night message and good-bye.
The days are stacked against
what we think we are:
near the raven rookery
inside the bend of river
with snowmelt and rain
flooding the bend; I've failed to stalk
these birds again and they flutter
and wheel above me with parental screams
saying, *Get out get out you bastard.*
The days are stacked against
what we think we are.
After a month of interior weeping
it occurred to me that in times like these
I have nothing to fall back on
except the sun and moon and earth.
I dress in camouflage and crawl
around swamps and forest, seeing
the bitch coyote five times but never
before she sees me. Her look
is curious, almost a smile.
The days are stacked against
what we think we are:

it is nearly impossible
to surprise ourselves.
I will never wake up
and be able to play the piano.
South fifteen miles, still
near the river, calling coyotes
with Dennis E: full moon in east,
northern lights in pale green swirl,
from the west an immense line squall
and thunderstorm approaching off Lake Superior.
Failing with his call he uses
the song of the loon to bring
an answer from the coyotes.
"They can't resist it," he says.
The days are stacked against
what we think we are.
Standing in the river up to my waist
the infant beaver peeks at me
from the flooded tag alder
and approaches though warned
by her mother whacking her tail.
About seven feet away she bobs
to dive, mooning me with her small
pink ass, rising again for another
look, then downward swimming
past my leg, still looking.
The days are finally stacked
against what we think we are:
how long can I stare at the river?
Three months in a row now
with no signs of stopping,
glancing to the right, an almost
embarrassed feeling that the river
will stop flowing and I can go home.

The days, at last, are stacked against
what we think we are.
Who in their most hallowed, sleepless
night with the moon seven feet
outside the window, the moon
that the river swallows, would wish
it otherwise?

On New Year's Eve I'm wrapped
in my habits, looking up to the TV
to see the red ball, the apple,
rise or fall, I forget which:
a poem on the cherry-wood table, a fire,
a blizzard, some whiskey, three
restless cats, and two sleeping dogs,
at home and making three gallons
of *menudo* for the revelers who'll
need it come tomorrow after amateur night:
about ten pounds of tripe, ancho,
molido, serrano, and chipotle peppers, cumin,
coriander, a few calves' or piglets' feet.
I don't wonder what is becoming
to the man already becoming.
I also added a half-quart of stock
left over from last night's *bollito misto*
wherein I poach for appropriate times:
fifteen pounds of veal bones to be discarded,
a beef brisket, a pork roast, Italian sausage,
a large barnyard hen, a pheasant, a guinea
hen, and for about thirty minutes until
rosy rare a whole filet, served with
three sauces: tomato coulis, piquante (anchovies & capers etc.)
and a rouille. Last week when my daughter
came home from NYC I made her venison

with truffles, also roast quail for Christmas
breakfast, also a wild turkey, some roast mallards & grouse,
also a cacciatore of rabbit & pheasant.
Oddly the best meal of the year
was in the cabin by the river:
a single fresh brook trout *au bleu*
with one boiled new potato and one
wild-leek vinaigrette. By the river
I try to keep alive, perhaps to write
more poems, though lately I think
of us all as lay-down comedians
who, when we finally tried to get up,
have found that our feet are mushy,
and what's more, no one cares
or bothers to read anymore those
sotto voce below-radar flights
from the empirical. But I am wrapped
in my habits. I must send my prayer
upward and downward. "Why do you write
poems?" the stewardess asked. "I guess
it's because every angel is terrible,
still though, alas, I invoke these almost
deadly birds of the soul,"
I cribbed from Rilke.

The travels on dry riverbeds: Salt River,
or nearly dry up Canyon de Chelly,
a half-foot of water—a skin over
the brown riverbed. The Navajo
family stuck with a load of dry
corn and crab apples. Only the woman
speaks English, the children at first shy
and frightened of my blind left eye
(some tribes attach importance to this —

strangely enough, this eye can see underwater).
We're up on the del Muerto fork and while
I'm kneeling in the water shoving rocks
under the axle I glance skyward
at an Anasazi cliff dwelling, the "ancient
ones" they're called. This morning
a young schizophrenic Navajo attacked
our truck with a club, his head seeming
to turn nearly all the way around as
an owl's. Finally the children smile
as the truck is pulled free. I am given
a hatful of the most delicious crab apples
in the world. I watch the first apple
core float west on the slender current,
my throat a knot of everything
I no longer understand.

Sitting on the bank, the water
stares back so deeply you can hear
it afterward when you wish. It is the water
of dreams, and for the nightwalker
who can almost walk on the water,
it is most of all the water of awakening,
passing with the speed of life
herself, drifting in circles in an eddy
joining the current again
as if the eddy were a few moments' sleep.

The story can't hesitate to stop.
I can't find a river in Los Angeles
except the cement one behind Sportsman's Lodge
on Ventura. There I feel my
high blood pressure like an electric tiara
around my head, a small comic cloud,

a miniature junkyard where my confused
desires, hopes, hates, and loves short circuit
in little puffs of hissing ozone. And the women
are hard green horses disappearing,
concealing themselves in buildings and tops
of wild palms in ambush.
A riverless city of redolent
and banal sobs, green girls
in trees, girls hard as basalt.
"My grandfather screwed me
when I was seven years old,"
she said, while I looked out
at the cement river flowing with dusty rain,
at three dogs playing in the cement river.
"He's dead now so there's no point
sweating it," she added.

Up in the Amazon River Basin
during a dark time Matthiessen built
a raft with a native, chewed some coca leaves,
boarded the raft and off they went on a river
not on any map, uncharted, wanting to see
the Great Mother of Snakes; a truncated
version of our voyage of seventy years –
actuarial average. To see green and live green,
moving on water sometimes clouded often clear.
Now our own pond is white with ice.
In the barnyard lying in the snow
I can hear the underground creek,
a creek without a name.

I forgot to tell you that while
I was away my heart broke
and I became not so much old, but older,

definably older within a few days.
This happened on a cold dawn in New Iberia
while I was feeding a frightened stray
dog a sack of pork rinds in the rain.

Three girls danced the "Cotton-Eyed Joe,"
almost sedate, erect, with relentless grace,
where did they come from
and where did they go
in ever-so-delicate circles?
And because of time, circles
that no longer close
or return to themselves.

I rode the gray horse
all day in the rain.
The fields became unmoving rivers,
the trees foreshortened.
I saw a girl in a white dress
standing half-hidden in the water
behind a maple tree.
I pretended not to notice
and made a long slow circle
behind a floating hedgetop
to catch her unawares.
She was gone but I had that prickly
fear someone was watching from a tree,
far up in a leaf-veil of green maple leaves.
Now the horse began swimming
toward higher ground, from where
I watched the tree until dark.

"Life, this vastly mysterious process
to which our culture inures us

lest we become useless citizens!
And is it terrible to be lonely and ill?"
she wrote. "Not at all, in fact, it is better
to be lonely when ill. To others, friends,
relatives, loved ones, death is our most
interesting, our most dramatic act.
Perhaps the best thing I've learned
from these apparently cursed and bedraggled
Indians I've studied all these years
is how to die. Last year I sat beside
a seven-year-old Hopi girl as she sang
her death song in a slight quavering
voice. Who among us whites, child
or adult, will sing while we die?"

On Whitefish Bay, the motor broke down
in heavy seas. We chopped ice off the gunwales
quite happily as it was unlikely we'd survive
and it was something to do. Ted just sat there
out of the wind and spray, drinking whiskey.
"I been on the wagon for a year. If I'm going
to die by god at least I get to have a drink."

What is it to actually go outside the nest
we have built for ourselves, and earlier
our father's nest: to go into a forest
alone with our eyes open? It's different
when you don't know what's over the hill —
keep the river on your left, then you see
the river on your right. I have simply
forgotten left and right, even up and down,
whirl then sleep on a cloudy day to forget
direction. It is hard to learn how
to be lost after so much training.

In New York I clocked
seven tugboats on the East River
in less than a half hour;
then I went to a party
where very rich people
talked about their arches,
foot arches, not architectural arches.
Back at my post I dozed
and saw only one more tugboat
before I slept.

But in New York I also saw a big hole
of maddened pipes with all the direction
of the swastika and a few immigrants
figuring it all out with the impenetrable
good sense of those who do the actual
work of the world.

How did I forget that rich turbulent
river, so cold in the rumply brown folds
of spring; by August cool, clear, glittery
in the sunlight; umbrous as it dips
under the logjam. In May, the river
a roar beyond a thin wall of sleep, with
the world of snow still gliding in rivulets
down imperceptible slopes; in August
through the screened window against which
bugs and moths scratch so lightly,
as lightly as the river sounds.

How can I renew oaths
I can't quite remember?
In New Orleans I was light in body and soul
because of food poisoning, the bathroom gymnastics

of flesh against marble floor,
seeing the underside of the bathtub
for the first time since I was a child,
and the next day crossing Cajun bridges
in the Atchafalaya, where blacks were thrown
to alligators I'm told, black souls whirling
in brown water, whirling
in an immaculate crawfish
rosary.

In the water I can remember
women I didn't know: Adriana
dancing her way home at the end
of a rope, a cool Tuscany night,
the apple tree in bloom;
the moon which I checked
was not quite full, a half-moon,
the rest of the life abandoned to the dark.

I warned myself all night
but then halfway between my ears
I turned toward the heavens
and reached the top of my head.
From there I can go just about
anywhere I want and I've never
found my way back home.

This isn't the old song
of the suicidal house,
I forgot the tune about small
windows growing smaller, the door
neither big enough to enter
nor exit, the sinking hydraulic ceilings
and the attic full of wet cement.

I wanted to go to the Camargue,
to Corsica, to return to Costa Rica,
but I couldn't escape the suicidal house
until May when I drove
through the snow to reach the river.

On the bank by the spring creek
my shadow seemed to leap
up to gather me, or it leapt
up to gather me, not seeming so
but as a natural fact. Faulkner said
that the drowned man's shadow had watched
him from the river all the time.

Drowning in the bourgeois trough,
a *bourride* or gruel of money, drugs,
whiskey, hotels, the dream coasts,
ass in the air at the trough, drowning
in a river of pus, pus of civilization,
pus of cities, unholy river of shit,
of filth, shit of nightmares, shit
of skewed dreams and swallowed years.
The river pulls me out,
draws me elsewhere
and down to blue water,
green water,
black water.

How far between the Virgin
and the Garrison and back?
Why is it a hundred times farther to get back,
the return upriver in the dark?
It isn't innocence, but to win back breath,
body heat, the light that gathers around

a waking animal. Ten years ago I saw
the dancing Virgin in a basement
in New York, a whirl of hot color
from floor to ceiling, whirling in a dance.
At eighteen in New York
on Grove Street I discovered
red wine, garlic, Rimbaud,
and a red-haired girl. Livid colors
not known in farm country,
also Charlie Parker, Sonny Rollins,
the odors from restaurant vents,
thirty-five-cent Italian sausages
on Macdougal, and the Hudson River:
days of river-watching and trying
to get on a boat for the tropics and see
that Great Ocean river, the Gulf Stream.
Another fifteen years before I saw
the Ocean river and the sharks hanging
under the sargassum weed lines,
a blue river in green water,
and the sharks staring back, sinking
down listlessly into darker water;
the torpor of heat, a hundred low-tide
nights begging a forgetfulness
I haven't quite earned.

I forgot where I heard that poems
are designed to waken sleeping gods;
in our time they've taken on nearly
unrecognizable shapes as gods will do;
one is a dog, one is a scarecrow
that doesn't work—crows perch
on the wind-whipped sleeves,
one is a carpenter who doesn't become Jesus,

one is a girl who went to heaven
sixty years early. Gods die,
and not always out of choice,
like near-sighted cats jumping
between buildings seven stories up.
One god drew feathers out of my skin
so I could fly, a favor close to terror.
But this isn't a map of the gods.
When they live in rivers
it's because rivers have no equilibrium;
gods resent equilibrium when everything
that lives *moves;* boulders
are a war of atoms, and the dandelion
cracks upward through the blacktop road.
Seltzer's tropical beetle grew
from a larval lump in a man's arm,
emerging full grown, pincers waving.
On Mt. Cuchama there were so many
gods passing through I hid in a hole
in a rock, waking one by accident.
I fled with a tight ass and cold skin.
I could draw a map of this place
but they're never caught in the same location
twice. And their voices change from involuntary
screams to the singular wail of the loon,
possibly the wind that can howl down Wall St.
Gods have long abandoned the banality of war
though they were stirred by a hundred-year-old
guitarist I heard in Brazil, also the autistic child
at the piano. We'll be greeted at death
so why should I wait? Today I invoked
any available god back in the woods in the fog.
The world was white with last week's melting
blizzard, the fog drifting upward, then descending.

The only sound was a porcupine eating bark
off an old tree, and a rivulet beneath the snow.
Sometimes the obvious is true: the full
moon on her bare bottom by the river!
For the gay, the full moon on the lover's prick!
Gods laugh at the fiction of gender.
Water-gods, moon-gods, god-fever,
sun-gods, fire-gods, give this earth-diver
more songs before I die.

A "system" suggests the cutting off,
i.e., in channel morphology, the reduction,
the suppression of texture to simplify:
to understand a man, or woman, growing
old with eagerness you first consider
the sensuality of death, an unacknowledged
surprise to most. In nature the physiology
has heat and color, beast and tree
saying aloud the wonder of death;
to study rivers, including the postcard
waterfalls, is to adopt another life;
a limited life attaches itself to the endless
movement, the renowned underground
rivers of South America which I've felt
thundering far beneath my feet—to die
is to descend into such rivers and flow
along in the perfect dark. But above ground
I'm memorizing life, from the winter moon
to the sound of my exhaustion in March
when all the sodden plans have collapsed
and only daughters, the dogs and cats
keep one from disappearing at gunpoint.
I brought myself here and stare nose to nose
at the tolerant cat who laps whiskey

from my mustache. Life often shatters
in schizoid splinters. I will avoid
becoming the cold stone wall I am straddling.

I had forgot what it was I liked
about life. I hear if you own a chimpanzee
they cease at a point to be funny. Writers
and politicians share an embarrassed moment
when they are sure all problems will disappear
if you get the language right.
That's not all they share—in each other's
company they are like boys who have been
discovered at wiener-play in the toilet.
At worst, it's the gift of gab.
At best it's Martin Luther King and Rimbaud.
Bearing down hard on love and death
there is an equal and opposite reaction.
All these years they have split the pie,
leaving the topping for the preachers
who don't want folks to fuck or eat.
What kind of magic, or rite of fertility,
to transcend this shit-soaked stew?

The river is as far as I can move
from the world of numbers: I'm all
for full retreats, escapes, a 47 yr. old runaway.
"Gettin' too old to run away," I wrote
but not quite believing this option is gray.
I stare into the deepest pool of the river
which holds the mystery of a cellar to a child,
and think of those two-track roads that dwindle
into nothing in the forest. I have this feeling
of walking around for days with the wind
knocked out of me. In the cellar was a root

cellar where we stored potatoes, apples, carrots
and where a family of harmless blacksnakes lived.
In certain rivers there are pools a hundred
foot deep. In a swamp I must keep secret
there is a deep boiling spring around which
in the dog days of August large brook trout
swim and feed. An adult can speak dreams
to children saying that there is a spring
that goes down to the center of the earth.
Maybe there is. Next summer I'm designing
and building a small river about seventy-seven
foot long. It will flow both ways, in reverse
of nature. I will build a dam and blow it up.

The involuntary image that sweeps
into the mind, irresistible and without evident
cause as a dream or thunderstorm,
or rising to the surface from childhood,
the longest journey taken in a split second,
from there to now, without pause:
in the woods with Mary Cooper, my first love
wearing a violet scarf in May. We're
looking after her huge mongoloid aunt,
trailing after this woman who loves us
but so dimly perceives the world. We pick
and clean wild leeks for her. The creek
is wild and dangerous with the last
of the snowmelt. The child-woman
tries to enter the creek and we tackle her.
She's stronger, then slowly understands,
half-wet and muddy. She kisses me
while Mary laughs, then Mary kisses me
over and over. Now I see the pools
in the Mongol eyes that watch and smile

with delight and hear the roar of the creek,
smell the scent of leeks on her muddy lips.

This is an obscene koan set plumb
in the middle of the Occident:
the man with three hands lacks symmetry
but claps the loudest, the chicken
in circles on the sideless road, a plane
that takes off and can never land.
I am not quite alert enough to live.
The fallen nest and fire in the closet,
my world without guardrails, the electric
noose, the puddle that had no bottom.
The fish in underground rivers are white
and blind as the porpoises who live far up
the muddy Amazon. In New York and LA
you don't want to see, hear, smell,
and you only open your mouth in restaurants.
At night you touch people with rock-hard skins.
I'm trying to become alert enough to live.
Yesterday after the blizzard I hiked far back
in a new swamp and found an iceless
pond connected to the river by a small creek.
Against deep white snow and black trees
there was a sulfurous fumarole, rank and sharp
in cold air. The water bubbled up brown,
then spread in turquoise to deep black,
without the track of a single mammal to drink.
This was nature's own, a beauty too strong
for life; a place to drown not live.

On waking after the accident
I was presented with the "whole picture"
as they say, magnificently detailed,

a child's diorama of what life appears to be:
staring at the picture I became drowsy
with relief when I noticed a yellow
dot of light in the lower right-hand corner.
I unhooked the machines and tubes and crawled
to the picture, with an eyeball to the dot
of light, which turned out to be a miniature
tunnel at the end of which I could see
mountains and stars whirling and tumbling,
sheets of emotions, vertical rivers, upside-
down lakes, herds of unknown mammals, birds
shedding feathers and regrowing them instantly,
snakes with feathered heads eating their own
shed skins, fish swimming straight up,
the bottom of Isaiah's robe, live whales
on dry ground, lions drinking from a golden
bowl of milk, the rush of night,
and somewhere in this the murmur of gods –
a tree-rubbing-tree music, a sweet howl
of water and rock-grating-rock, fire
hissing from fissures, the moon settled
comfortably on the ground, beginning to roll.

THE BRAND NEW STATUE OF LIBERTY

to Lee Iacocca (another Michigan boy)

I was commissioned in a dream by Imanja,
also the Black Pope of Brazil, Tancred,
to design a seven-tiered necklace
of seven thousand skulls for the Statue of Liberty.
Of course from a distance they'll look
like pearls, but in November
when the strongest winds blow, the skulls
will rattle wildly, bone against metal,
a crack and chatter of bone against metal,
the true sound of history, this metal striking bone.
I'm not going to get heavy-handed –
a job is a job and I've leased a football
field for the summer, gathered a group of ladies
who are art lovers, leased in advance
a bull Sikorsky freight helicopter
to drop on the necklace: funding comes
from Ford Foundation, Rockefeller, the NEA.
There is one Jewish skull from Atlanta, two
from Mississippi, but this is basically
an indigenous cast except skulls from tribes
of blacks who got a free ride over from Africa,
representative skulls from all the Indian
tribes, an assortment of grizzly, wolf,
coyote and buffalo skulls. But what beauty
when the morning summer sun glances
off these bony pates! And her great
iron lips quivering in a smile, almost a smirk
so that she'll drop the torch to fondle the jewels.

MY FRIEND THE BEAR

Down in the bone myth of the cellar
of this farmhouse, behind the empty fruit jars
the whole wall swings open to the room
where I keep the bear. There's a tunnel
to the outside on the far wall that emerges
in the lilac grove in the backyard
but she rarely uses it, knowing there's no room
around here for a freewheeling bear.
She's not a dainty eater so once a day
I shovel shit while she lopes in playful circles.
Privately she likes religion—from the bedroom
I hear her incantatory moans and howls
below me—and April 23rd, when I open
the car trunk and whistle at midnight
and she shoots up the tunnel, almost airborne
when she meets the night. We head north
and her growls are less friendly as she scents
the forest-above-the-road smell. I release
her where I found her as an orphan three
years ago, bawling against the dead carcass
of her mother. I let her go at the head
of the gully leading down to the swamp,
jumping free of her snarls and roars.
But each October 9th, one day before bear season
she reappears at the cabin frightening
the bird dogs. We embrace ear to ear,
her huge head on my shoulder,
her breathing like god's.

COUNTING BIRDS

for Gerald Vizenor

As a child, fresh out of the hospital
with tape covering the left side
of my face, I began to count birds.
At age fifty the sum total is precise
and astonishing, my only secret.
Some men count women or the cars
they've owned, their shirts –
long sleeved and short sleeved –
or shoes, but I have my birds,
excluding, of course, those extraordinary
days: the twenty-one thousand
snow geese and sandhill cranes at
Bosque del Apache; the sky blinded
by great frigate birds in the Pacific
off Anconcito, Ecuador; the twenty-one
thousand pink flamingos in Ngorongoro Crater
in Tanzania; the vast flock of seabirds
on the Seri coast of the Sea of Cortez
down in Sonora that left at nightfall,
then reappeared, resuming
their exact positions at dawn;
the one thousand cliff swallows nesting
in the sand cliffs of Pyramid Point,
their small round burrows like eyes,
really the souls of the Anasazi who flew
here a thousand years ago
to wait the coming of the Manitou.
And then there were the usual, almost deadly
birds of the soul—the crow with silver
harness I rode one night as if she

were a black, feathered angel;
the birds I became to escape unfortunate
circumstances—how the skin ached
as the feathers shot out toward light;
the thousand birds the dogs helped
me shoot to become a bird (grouse, woodcock,
duck, dove, snipe, pheasant, prairie chicken, etc.).
On my deathbed I'll write this secret
number on a slip of paper and pass
it to my wife and two daughters.
It will be a hot evening in late June
and they might be glancing out the window
at the thunderstorm's approach from the west.
Looking past their eyes and a dead fly
on the window screen I'll wonder
if there's a bird waiting for me in the onrushing clouds.
O birds, I'll sing to myself, *you've carried*
me along on this bloody voyage,
carry me now into that cloud,
into the marvel of this final night.

After Ikkyū and Other Poems

| 1996

AFTER IKKYŪ

1

Our minds buzz like bees
but not the bees' minds.
It's just wings not heart
they say, moving to another flower.

6

Shoju sat all night in the graveyard
among wolves who sniffed his Adam's apple.
First light moving in the air
he arose, peed, and ate breakfast.

11

At Hard Luck Ranch the tea is hot,
the sky's dark blue. Behind me
the jaguar skin from the jaguar
who died so long ago from a bullet
while perched on a calf's back
tells me the same old story.

12

Not here and now but now and here.
If you don't know the difference
is a matter of life and death, get down
naked on bare knees in the snow
and study the ticking of your watch.

13

The hound I've known for three years
trots down the mountain road
with a nod at me, pretending he knows
what he's doing miles from home
on a sunlit morning. He's headed
for a kind of place he hasn't quite found yet
and might not recognize when he gets there.

14

At the strip club in Lincoln, Nebraska,
she said, "I'm the Princess of Shalimar."
Doubtless, I thought, at a loss for words
but not images, the air moist but without
the promise of a rain. She's not bending
pinkly like a pretzel but a body.
At this age, my first bona fide royalty.

15

Way up a sandy draw in the foothills
of the Whetstone Mountains I found cougar
tracks so fresh, damp sand was still
trickling in from the edges. For some reason
I knelt and sniffed them, quite sure
I was being watched by a living rock
in the vast, heat-blurred landscape.

18

My *zabuton* doubles as a dog bed. Rose sleeps
there, full to the fur with *mu*. Glanced in
on a moonlit night; her slight white figure coiled

on the green cushion, shaking with quail dreams.
Sensing me, an eye opens, single tail-wag. Back to sleep.
When she's awake, she's so awake I'm ashamed
of my own warm water dance, my sitting too long at the fire.

24

The monk is eighty-seven. There's no fat
left on his feet to defend against stones.
He forgot his hat, larger in recent years.
By a creek he sees a woman he saw fifty summers
before, somehow still a girl to him. Once again his hands
tremble when she gives him a tin cup of water.

29

The four seasons, the ten oaths, the nine colors, three vowels
that stretch forth their paltry hands to the seven flavors
and the one money, the official parody of prayer.
Up on this mountain, stumbling on talus, on the north face
there is snow, and on the south, buds of pink flowers.

37

Beware, o wanderer, the road is walking too,
said Rilke one day to no one in particular
as good poets everywhere address the six directions.
If you can't bow, you're dead meat. You'll break
like uncooked spaghetti. Listen to the gods.
They're shouting in your ear every second.

39

In the next installment I'll give you Crazy Horse and Anne Frank,
their conversation as recorded by Matthew of Gospel fame,
who was wont, as all scriveners, to add a bit of this and that.
God is terse. The earth's proper scripture could be carried
on a three-by-five card if we weren't drunk on our own blood.

40

Walking the lakeshore at first moonlight I can see
feathers, stones, smooth spars, seaweed,
and the doe washed up from the Manitou two days ago
has been nearly eaten by the coyotes and ravens
I poke my stick in the moon's watery face, then apologize.

50

If I'm not mistaken, everyone seems to go back
to where they came from, ending up right
where they began. Our beloved cat died today.
She liked to sit on my head during *zazen*
back when she was a child. I bow to her magnificence
beside which all churches and temples are privy holes.

57

Took my own life because I was permanently crippled,
put on backward, the repairs eating up money and time.
For fifty-seven years I've had it all wrong
until I studied the other side of the mirror.
No birth before death. The other way around.
How pleasant to get off a horse in the middle of the lake.

THE DAVENPORT LUNAR ECLIPSE

Overlooking the Mississippi
I never thought I'd get this old.
It was mostly my confusion about time
and the moon, and seeing the lovely way
homely old men treat their homely old women
in Nebraska and Iowa, the lunch-time
touch over green Jell-O with pineapple
and fried "fish rectangles" for $2.95.
When I passed Des Moines the radio said
there were long lines to see the entire cow
sculpted out of butter. The earth is right smack
between the sun and the moon, the black waitress
told me at the Salty Pelican on the waterfront,
home from wild Houston to nurse her sick dad.
My good eye is burning up from fatigue
as it squints up above the Mississippi
where the moon is losing its edge to black.
It likely doesn't know what's happening to it,
I thought, pressed down to my meal and wine
by a fresh load of incomprehension.
My grandma lived in Davenport in the 1890s
just after Wounded Knee, a signal event,
the beginning of America's *Sickness unto Death*.
I'd like to nurse my father back to health
he's been dead thirty years, I said
to the waitress who agreed. That's why she
came home, she said, you only got one.
Now I find myself at fifty-one in Davenport
and drop the issue right into the Mississippi
where it is free to swim with the moon's reflection.
At the bar there are two girls of incomprehensible beauty

for the time being, as Swedish as my Grandma,
speaking in bad grammar as they listen to a band
of middle-aged Swede saxophonists braying
"Bye-Bye Blackbird" over and over, with a clumsy
but specific charm. The girls fail to notice me –
perhaps I should give them the thousand dollars
in my wallet but I've forgotten just how.
I feel pleasantly old and stupid, deciding
not to worry about who I am but how I spend
my days, until I tear in the weak places
like a thin, worn sheet. Back in my room
I can't hear the river passing like time,
or the moon emerging from the shadow of earth,
but I can see the water that never repeats itself.
It's very difficult to look at the World
and into your heart at the same time.
In between, a life has passed.

BEAR

Bear died standing up,
paws on log,
howling. Shot
right through the heart.

The hunter only wanted the head,
the hide. I ate her
so she wouldn't go to waste,
dumped naked in a dump,
skinless, looking like ourselves
if we had been flayed,
red as death.

Now there are bear dreams
again for the bear-eater: O god,
the bears have come down the hill,
bears from everywhere on earth,
all colors, sizes, filtering
out of the woods behind the cabin.

A half-mile up
I plummeted toward the river to die,
pushed there. Then pinions creaked;
I flew downstream until I clutched
a white pine, the mind stepping back
to see half-bird, half-bear,
waking in the tree to wet
fur and feathers.

Hotei and bear
sitting side by side,

disappear into each other.
Who is to say
which of us is one?

We loaded the thousand-pound logs
by hand, the truck swaying.
Paused to caress my friend and helper,
the bear beside me, eye to eye,
breath breathing breath.

And now tonight, a big blue
November moon. Startled to find myself
wandering the edge of a foggy
tamarack marsh, scenting the cold
wet air, delicious in the moonglow.
Scratched against swart hemlock,
an itch to give it all up, shuffling
empty-bellied toward home, the yellow
square of cabin light between trees,
the human shape of yellow light,
to turn around,
to give up again this human shape.

TWILIGHT

For the first time
far in the distance
he could see his twilight
wrapping around the green hill
where three rivers start,
and sliding down toward him
through the trees until it reached
the blueberry marsh and stopped,
telling him to go away, not now,
not for the time being.

RETURN TO YESENIN

25 years later

> For only in praising is my heart still mine, so violently
> do I know the world.
> RAINER MARIA RILKE, *Fragment of an Elegy*

I forgot to say that at the moment of death Yesenin
stood there like a misty-eyed pioneer woman trying
to figure out what happened. Were the children
still in the burning barn with the bawling cows?
He was too sensitive for words, and the idea of a rope
was a wound he couldn't stop picking at. To step
back from this swinging man twisting clockwise
is to see how we mine ourselves too deeply,
that way down there we can break through the soul's
rock into a black underground river that sweeps us away.
To be frank, I'd rather live to feed my dogs,
knowing the world says *no* in ten thousand ways
and *yes* in only a few. The dogs don't need another
weeping Jesus on the cross of Art, strumming the scars
to keep them alive, tending them in a private
garden as if our night-blooming tumors were fruit.
I let you go for twenty years and am now only
checking to see that you are really dead. There was an urge
to put a few bullets through Nixon's coffin or a big,
sharp wooden stake, and a girl told me she just saw
Jimi Hendrix at an AIDS benefit in Santa Monica.
How could I disbelieve her when her nipples
were rosebuds, though you had to avoid the snakes
in her hair. If you had hanged yourself in Argentina
you would have twisted counterclockwise. We can't
ask if it was worth it, can we? Any more than we can

ask a whale its mother's name. Too bad we couldn't
go to Mexico together and croak a few small gods
back to life. I've entered my third act and am
still following my songs on that thin line between
woods and field, well short of the mouth of your hell.

The Shape of the Journey:
New and Collected Poems

| 1998

I

I can hear the cow dogs sleeping
in the dust, the windmill's
creak above thirty-three
sets of shrill mating birds.
The vultures fly above the corrals
so softly the air ignores them.
In all of the eons, past and future,
not one day clones itself.

7

O that girl, only young men
dare to look at her directly
while I manage the most sidelong of glances:
olive-skinned with a Modigliani throat,
lustrous obsidian hair, the narrowest
of waists and high French bottom, ample
breasts she tries to hide in a loose blouse.
Though Latina her profile is from a Babylonian
frieze and when she walks her small white dog
with brown spots she fairly floats along,
looking neither left nor right, meeting no one's
glance as if beauty was a curse. In the grocery
store when I drew close her scent was jacaranda,
the tropical flower that makes no excuses.
This geezer's heart swells stupidly to the dampish
promise. I walk too often in the cold shadow
of the mountain wall up the arroyo behind the house.
Empty pages are dry ice, numbing the hands and heart.

If I weep I do so in the shower so that no one,
not even I, can tell. To see her is to feel
time's cold machete against my grizzled neck,
puzzled that again beauty has found her home in threat.

10

I know a private mountain range with a big bowl in its center that
you find by following the narrowest creek bed, sometimes crawling
until you struggle through a thicket until you reach two large cupped
hands of stone in the middle of which is a hill, a promontory, which
would be called a mountain back home. There is iron in this hill and
it sucks down summer lightning, thousands and thousands of strokes
through time, shattering the gigantic top into a field of undramatic
crystals that would bring a buck a piece at a rock show. I was here in
a dark time and stood there and said, "I have put my poem in order
on the threshold of my tongue," quoting someone from long, long
ago, then got the hell off the mountain due to tremors of undeter-
mined source. Later that night sleeping under an oak a swarm of elf
owls (*Micrathene whitneyi*) descended to a half-dozen feet above my
head and a thousand white sycamores undulated in the full moon,
obviously the living souls of lightning strokes upside down along
the arroyo bed. A modern man, I do not make undue connections
though my heart wrenches daily against the unknowable, almighty
throb and heave of the universe against my skin that sings a song for
which we haven't quite found the words.

11

Today the warblers undulate
fishlike, floating down,
lifting up with wing beats
while below me in the creek
minnows undulate birdlike,

floating down, lifting up with fin beats.
For a minute I lose the sense
of up and down.

16

My favorite stump straddles a gully a dozen
miles from any human habitation.
My eschatology includes scats, animal poop,
scatology so that when I nestle under this stump
out of the rain I see the scats of bear, bobcat,
coyote. I won't say that I feel at home
under this vast white pine stump, the roots
spread around me, so large in places no arms
can encircle them, as if you were under the body
of a mythic spider, the thunder ratcheting
the sky so that the earth hums beneath you.
Here is a place to think about nothing,
which is what I do. If the rain beats down
hard enough tiny creeks form beside my shit-strewn
pile of sand. The coyote has been eating mice,
the bear berries, the bobcat a rabbit. It's dry
enough so it doesn't smell except for ancient
wet wood and gravel, pine pitch, needles. Luckily
a sandhill crane nests nearby so that in June
if I doze I'm awakened by her cracked
and prehistoric cry, waking startled, feeling
the two million years I actually am.

29

How can I be alone when these brain cells
chat to me their million messages
a minute. But sitting there in the ordinary

trance that is any mammal's birthright, say on a desert
boulder or northern stump, a riverbank,
we can imitate a barrel cactus, a hemlock tree,
the water that flows through time as surely
as ourselves. The mind loses its distant
machine-gun patter, becomes a frog's
occasional croak. A trout's last jump in the dark,
a horned owl's occasional hoot,
or in the desert alone at night
the voiceless stars light my primate
fingers that I lift up to curl
around their bright cosmic bodies.

34
Not how many different birds I've seen
but how many have seen me,
letting the event go unremarked
except for the quietest sense of malevolence,
dead quiet, then restarting their lives
after fear, not with song, which is reserved
for lovers, but the harsh and quizzical
chatter with which we all get by:
but if she or he passes by and the need
is felt we hear the music that transcends all fear,
and sometimes the simpler songs that greet sunrise,
rain or twilight. Here I am.
They sing what and where they are.

Braided Creek:
A Conversation in Poetry

| 2003

Braided Creek: A Conversation in Poetry was cowritten with Ted Kooser and contains more than three hundred short poems, with no indication of who wrote which poem. When asked about attributions for the individual poems, Jim Harrison said in an interview, "Everyone gets tired of this continuing cult of the personality. This book is an assertion in favor of poetry and against credentials." In honor of *conversation,* and realizing that none of these poems would exist without a friend to talk with, I simply selected essential poems from *Braided Creek* and marveled at the harmonies. —JB

While my bowl is still half full,
you can eat out of it too,
and when it is empty,
just bury it out in the flowers.

All those years
I had in my pocket.
I spent them,
nickel-and-dime.

The Pilot razor-point pen is my
compass, watch, and soul chaser.
Thousands of miles of black squiggles.

For sixty-three years I've ground myself
within this karmic mortar. Yesterday I washed
it out and put it high on the pantry shelf.

Republicans think that all over the world
darker-skinned people are having more fun
than they are. It's largely true.

Everyone thought I'd die
in my twenties, thirties, forties, fifties.
This can't go on forever.

Throw out the anchor
unattached to a rope.

Heart lifts as it sinks.
Out of my mind at last.

When we were very poor one spring
I fished a snowy river and caught
a big trout. It changed our lives
that day: eating, drinking, singing, dancing.

Years ago
when I became tough as a nail
I became a nail.

I want to describe my life in hushed tones
like a TV nature program. *Dawn in the north.*
His nose stalks the air for newborn coffee.

Some days
one needs to hide
from possibility.

Each time I go outside the world
is different. This has happened
all my life.

Fear is a swallow
in a boarded-up warehouse,
seeking a window out.

On its stand on the empty stage
the tuba with its big brass ear
enjoys the silence.

So what if women
no longer smile to see me?
I smile to see them!

Why do I behave so badly?
Just because. That's still
a good answer.

Open the shoe-store door
and a bell rings:
two shoehorns on a shoelace.

Let go of the mind, the thousand blue
story fragments we tell ourselves
each day to keep the world underfoot.

I trace my noble ancestry back
to the first seed, the first cell
that emerged reluctantly from the void.

A nephew rubs the sore feet
of his aunt,
and the rope that lifts us all toward grace
creaks in the pulley.

An empty boat
will volunteer for anything.

Gentle readers, tomorrow I undergo
radical brain surgery, but don't worry.
Win some. Lose some. Mostly ties.

Wanted: Looking for owl roosts
for pellets for Science project.
Call Marli.

In each of my cells Dad and Mom
are still doing their jobs. As always,
Dad says *yes,* Mom says *no.* I split the difference
and feel deep sympathy for my children.

At the tip of memory's
great funnel-cloud
is the nib of a pen.

Strange world indeed:
a poet keeping himself awake
to write about insomnia.

The sparrow is not busy,
but hungry.

I might have been a welder,
kneeling at a fountain of sparks
in my mask of stars.

After carefully listing my 10,000 illusions
I noticed that nearly all that I found
in the depths was lost in the shallows.

If you can awaken
inside the familiar
and discover it strange
you need never leave home.

You told me you couldn't see
a better day coming,
so I gave you my eyes.

The way a springer spaniel
hops through deep grass,
I was once a lover like that.

When she left me
I stood out in the thunderstorm,
hoping to be destroyed by lightning.
It missed, first left, then right.

When a hammer sings
its head is loose.

I grow older.
I still like women, but mostly
I like Mexican food.

Sleeping on my right side I think
of God. On my left side, sex.
On my back I snore with my dog.

The face you look out of
is never the face
your lover looks into.

The firefly's one word:
darkness!

One grows tired of the hoax of up
and down. Jesus descended into a universe
of neither perfect lines, squares, nor circles.

This slender blue thread,
if anything,
connects everything.

At my age,
even in airports,
why would you wish
time to move faster?

The clock stopped at 5:30 for three months.
Now it's always time to quit work,
have a drink, cook dinner.

On my desk two
indisputably great creations:
duct tape and saltine crackers.

Suddenly my clocks agree.
One has been stopped for several
months, but twice a day
they have this tender moment.

In deer season,
walking in the woods,
I sing like Pavarotti.

"What I would do for wisdom,"
I cried out as a young man.
Evidently not much. Or so it seems.
Even on walks I follow the dog.

After rowing my blue and brown boat
for three hours I liked the world again,
the two loons close by, the theory of red wine.

In 1947 a single gold nugget was found
hereabouts. Old men still look for a second one.
In between life has passed.

When I watched her hands
as she peeled a potato,
I gave up everything I owned.

I woke up as nothing. Now start piling
it on. No. Yes. No. Maybe. Indoors.
Outdoors. Me. You. Her corpse said stop.

Life has always yelled at me,
"Get your work done." At least
that's what I think she says.

The old Finn (85) walks
twenty-five miles to see his brother.
Why? "I don't have no car."

What if everyone you've loved
were still alive? That's the province
of the young, who don't know it.

Oh, to be in love,
with all five buckets
of the senses
overflowing!

The old hen scratches
then looks, scratches then looks.
My life.

I hope there's time
for this and that,
and not just this.

The butterfly's brain,
the size of a grain of salt,
guides her to Mexico.

Buddhists say everything is led by mind.
My doubts are healed by drinking
a bottle of red wine in thirty-three minutes.

I'm sixty-two and can drop dead
at any moment. Thinking this in August
I kissed the river's cold moving lips.

Come to think of it,
there's no reason to decide
who you are.

Stars from horizon to horizon.
A whole half universe
just to light the path.

Imagine a gallery
where all the paintings
opened and closed their wings!

Sometimes all it takes
to be happy
is a dime on the sidewalk.

The moon put her hand
over my mouth and told me
to shut up and watch.

I thought my friend was drinking
too much, but it was the vodka
that was drinking him.

So the Greeks had amphorae
with friezes of nymphs.
We have coffee mugs with ads
for farm equipment!

How is it the rich always know
what is best for the poor?

Like an old dog
I slowly lower and arrange myself
in a heap of sighs.

Foolish me,
to think my wine
would never turn.

Come close to death
and you begin to see
what's under your nose.

Alone in the car
we try to tell ourselves
some good news.

In our October windfall time red
apples on frostbitten green grass.
You learn to eat around the wormholes.

Treasure what you find
already in your pocket, friend.

Today a pink rose in a vase
on the table.
Tomorrow, petals.

Saving Daylight

| 2006

WATER

Before I was born I was water.
I thought of this sitting on a blue
chair surrounded by pink, red, white
hollyhocks in the yard in front
of my green studio. There are conclusions
to be drawn but I can't do it anymore.
Born man, child man, singing man,
dancing man, loving man, old man,
dying man. This is a round river
and we are her fish who become water.

CABBAGE

If only I had the genius of a cabbage
or even an onion to grow myself
in their laminae from the holy core
that bespeaks the final shape. Nothing
is outside of us in this overinterpreted world.
Bruises are the mouths of our perceptions.
The gods who have died are able to come
to life again. It's their secret that they wish
to share if anyone knows that they exist.
Belief is a mood that weighs nothing on anyone's
scale but nevertheless exists. The moose
down the road wears the black cloak of a god
and the dead bird lifts from a bed of moss
in a shape totally unknown to us.
It's after midnight in Montana.
I test the thickness of the universe, its resilience
to carry us further than any of us wish to go.
We shed our shapes slowly like moving water,
which ends up as it will so utterly far from home.

MOM AND DAD

Gentle readers, feel your naked belly button where
you were tied to your mother. Kneel and thank
her for your jubilant but woebegone life. Don't
for a moment think of the mood of your parents
when you were conceived which so vitally affects
your destiny. You have no control over that and
it's unprofitable to wonder if they were pissed
off or drunk, bored, watching television news,
listening to country music, or hopefully out in
the orchard grass feeling the crunch of wind-
fall apples under their frantic bodies.

NIGHT DHARMA

How restlessly the Buddha sleeps
between my ears, dreaming his dreams
of emptiness, writing his verbless poems.
(I almost rejected "green tree
white goat red sun blue sea.")
Verbs are time's illusion, he says.

In the stillness that surrounds us
we think we have to probe our wounds,
but with what? Mind caresses mind
not by saying *no* or *yes* but *neither.*

Turn your watch back to your birth
for a moment, then way ahead beyond
any expectation. There never was a coffin
worth a dime. These words emerge
from the skin as the sweat of gods
who drink only from the Great Mother's breasts.

Buddha sleeps on, disturbed when I disturb
him from his liquid dreams of blood and bone.
Without comment he sees the raven carrying
off the infant snake, the lovers' foggy
gasps, the lion's tongue that skins us.

One day we dozed against a white pine stump
in a world of dogwood and sugar plum blossoms.
An eye for an eye, he said, trading
a left for my right, the air green tea
in the sky's blue cup.

I forgot long division but does one
go into sixty-six more than sixty-six times?
There's the mother, two daughters, eight dogs,
I can't name all the cats and horses, a farm
for thirty-five years, then Montana, a cabin,
a border casita, two grandsons, two sons-in-law,
and graced by the sun and the moon, red wine
and garlic, lakes and rivers, the millions of trees.
I can't help but count out of habit, the secret
door underneath the vast stump where I founded
the usual Cro-Magnon religion, a door
enveloped by immense roots through which one day
I watched the passing legs of sandhill cranes,
napping where countless bears have napped,
an aperture above where the sky and the gods
may enter, yet I'm without the courage to watch
the full moon through this space. I can't figure
out a life. We're groundlings who wish to fly.
I live strongly in the memories of my dead dogs.
It's just a feeling that memories float around
waiting to be caught. I miss the cat that perched
on my head during *zazen*. Since my brother died
I've claimed the privilege of speaking to local rocks,
trees, birds, the creek. Last night a broad moonbeam
fell across my not-so-sunken chest. The smallest
gods ask me what there is beyond consciousness,
the moment by moment enclosure the mind
builds to capture the rudiments of time.
Two nights ago I heard a woman from across
the creek, a voice I hadn't heard since childhood.
I didn't answer. Red was red this dawn

after a night of the swirling milk of stars
that came too close. I felt lucky not to die.
My brother died at high noon one day in Arkansas.
Divide your death by your life and you get
a circle, though I'm not so good at math.
This morning I sat in the dirt playing
with five cow dogs, giving out a full pail of biscuits.

ANGRY WOMEN

Women in peignoirs are floating around
the landscape well out of eyesight
let alone reach. They are as palpable
as the ghost of my dog Rose whom I see
on long walks, especially when exhausted
and my half-blind eyes are blurred by cold wind
or sleet or snow. The women we've mistreated
never forgive us nor should they, thus their ghostly
energies thrive at dawn and twilight in this vast
country where any of the mind's movies can be played
against this rumpled wide-screened landscape.
Our souls are travelers. You can tell when your own
is gone, and then these bleak, improbable
visits from others, their dry tears because you were
never what you weren't, so that the world
becomes only what it is, the unforgiving flow
of an unfathomable river. Still they wanted you otherwise,
closer to their dreamchild, just as you imagined
fair maidens tight to you as decals to guide
you toward certainties. The new pup, uncrippled by ideals,
leaps against the fence, leaps at the mountains beyond.

ALCOHOL

In the far back room of the school
for young writers are two big illegal
formaldehyde glass jars holding the kidneys
and livers of Faulkner and Hemingway
among the tens of thousands of empty bottles
of everything they drank to fuel themselves
through their bloody voyages. Alive, their arms
were crooked out as question marks trying
to encircle the world. Dead, they are crazy
old men who convinced us of the reasonableness
of their tales, their books deducted from their caskets
at the last possible moment. And now we hold
them tightly as if they ever truly cared.
No one should wish to enter this room
but still some of us hurl ourselves against
the invisible door as if our stories and alcohol
were Siamese twins ineluctably joined at the head,
our hearts enlarged until they can barely beat.

FLOWER, 2001

Near a flowershop off boulevard Raspail
a woman in a sundress bending over,
I'd guess about 49 years of age
in a particular bloom, just entering
the early autumn of her life,
a thousand-year-old smile on her face
so wide open that I actually shuddered
the same shudder I did in 1989
coming over the lip of a sand dune
and seeing a big bear below me.

MOTHER NIGHT

When you wake at three a.m. you don't think
of your age or sex and rarely your name
or the plot of your life which has never
broken itself down into logical pieces.
At three a.m. you have the gift of incomprehension
wherein the galaxies make more sense
than your job or the government. Jesus at the well
with Mary Magdalene is much more vivid
than your car. You can clearly see the bear
climb to heaven on a golden rope in the children's
story no one ever wrote. Your childhood horse
named June still stomps the ground for an apple.
What is morning and what if it doesn't arrive?
One morning Mother dropped an egg and asked
me if God was the same species as we are?
Smear of light at five a.m. Sound of Weber's
sheep flock and sandhill cranes across the road,
burble of irrigation ditch beneath my window.
She said, "Only lunatics save newspapers
and magazines," fried me two eggs, then said,
"If you want to understand mortality look at birds."
Blue moon, two full moons this month,
which I conclude are two full moons. In what
direction do the dead fly off the earth?
Rising sun. A thousand blackbirds pronounce day.

BIRDS AGAIN

A secret came a week ago though I already
knew it just beyond the bruised lips of consciousness.
The very alive souls of thirty-five hundred dead birds
are harbored in my body. It's not uncomfortable.
I'm only temporary habitat for these not-quite-
weightless creatures. I offered a wordless invitation
and now they're roosting within me, recalling
how I had watched them at night
in fall and spring passing across earth moons,
little clouds of black confetti, chattering and singing
on their way north or south. Now in my dreams
I see from the air the rumpled green and beige,
the watery face of earth as if they're carrying
me rather than me carrying them. Next winter
I'll release them near the estuary west of Alvarado
and south of Veracruz. I can see them perching
on undiscovered Olmec heads. We'll say goodbye
and I'll return my dreams to earth.

POEM OF WAR (I)

The old rancher of seventy-nine years
said while branding and nutting young bulls
with the rank odor of burned hairs and flesh
in the air, the oil-slippery red nuts
plopping into a galvanized bucket,
"This smells just like Guadalcanal."

FENCE LINE TREE

There's a single tree at the fence line
here in Montana, a little like a tree
in the Sandhills of Nebraska, which may be miles
away. When I cross the unfertile pasture strewn
with rocks and the holes of gophers, badgers, coyotes,
and the rattlesnake den (a thousand killed
in a decade because they don't mix well with dogs
and children) in an hour's walking and reach
the tree, I find it oppressive. Likely it's
as old as I am, withstanding its isolation,
all gnarled and twisted from its battle
with weather. I sit against it until we merge,
and when I return home in the cold, windy
twilight I feel I've been gone for years.

In Search of Small Gods

| 2009

I BELIEVE

I believe in steep drop-offs, the thunderstorm across the lake
in 1949, cold winds, empty swimming pools,
the overgrown path to the creek, raw garlic,
used tires, taverns, saloons, bars, gallons of red wine,
abandoned farmhouses, stunted lilac groves,
gravel roads that end, brush piles, thickets, girls
who haven't quite gone totally wild, river eddies,
leaky wooden boats, the smell of used engine oil,
turbulent rivers, lakes without cottages lost in the woods,
the primrose growing out of a cow skull, the thousands
of birds I've talked to all of my life, the dogs
that talked back, the Chihuahuan ravens that follow
me on long walks. The rattler escaping the cold hose,
the fluttering unknown gods that I nearly see
from the left corner of my blind eye, struggling
to stay alive in a world that grinds them underfoot.

CALENDARS

Back in the blue chair in front of the green studio
another year has passed, or so they say, but calendars lie.
They're a kind of cosmic business machine like
their cousin clocks but break down at inopportune times.
Fifty years ago I learned to jump off the calendar
but I kept getting drawn back on for reasons
of greed and my imperishable stupidity.
Of late I've escaped those fatal squares
with their razor-sharp numbers for longer and longer.
I had to become the moving water I already am,
falling back into the human shape in order
not to frighten my children, grandchildren, dogs and friends.
Our old cat doesn't care. He laps the water where my face used to be.

LARSON'S HOLSTEIN BULL

Death waits inside us for a door to open.
Death is patient as a dead cat.
Death is a doorknob made of flesh.
Death is that angelic farm girl
gored by the bull on her way home
from school, crossing the pasture
for a shortcut. In the seventh grade
she couldn't read or write. She wasn't a virgin.
She was "simpleminded," we all said.
It was May, a time of lilacs and shooting stars.
She's lived in my memory for sixty years.
Death steals everything except our stories.

NEW MOON

Why does the new moon give anyone hope?
Nevertheless it does and always has for me
and likely does for that Mexican poet with no pesos,
maybe a couple of tortillas, chewing them while sitting
on a smooth rock beside a creek in the Sierra Madres
seeing the new moon tilted delicately away from Venus,
the faint silver light, the ever-so-small sliver
of white enamel rippling in the creek, the same moon,
he thinks, that soothed the Virgin in her great doubt
over the swollen belly beneath her breasts.
The fatherless son had two new moons in his forty days
in the wilderness, the second one telling him it was time
to become God and enter the beast of history.
This poet, though, ignores the sacraments of destiny
and only wants a poem to sing the liquid gift of night.

THE GOLDEN WINDOW

By accident my heart lifted with a rush.
Gone for weeks, finally home on a darkish day
of blustery wind, napped, waking in a few minutes
and the sun had come clean and crept around the house,
this light from one of trillions of stars
falling through the window skeined
by the willow's greenish bright yellow leaves
so that my half-asleep head opened wide
for the first time in many months, a cold sunstroke,
so yellow-gold, so gold-yellow, yellow-gold,
this eye beyond age bathed in yellow light.

—

Seventy days on the river with a confusion between
river turbulence and human tribulation. We are here
to be curious not consoled. The gift of the gods
is consciousness not my forlorn bleating prayers
for equilibrium, the self dog-paddling in circles
on its own algae-lidded pond. Emily Walter wrote:
    "We are given rivers so we know our hearts
    can break, but still keep us breathing."

—

When you run through the woods blindfolded
you're liable to collide with trees, I thought
one hot afternoon on the river. You can't drown yourself
if you swim well. We saw some plovers
and then a few yellowlegs with their peculiar cries,
and I remembered a very cold, windy September day
with Matthiessen and Danny when the birds lifted
me far out of myself. It was so cold and blustery the avian

world descended into the river valley and while fishing
we saw a golden eagle, two immature and two adult
bald eagles, two prairie falcons, two peregrines, Cooper's
hawks, two Swainson's, a sharp-shinned,
a rough-legged, a harrier, five turkey vultures,
three ospreys, and also saw buffleheads, wigeon,
teal, mallards, mourning doves, kingfishers,
ring-billed gulls, killdeer, spotted plovers,
sandpipers and sandhill cranes.
They also saw us. If a peregrine sees fifty times better
than we, what do we look like to them?
Unanswerable.

—

Nearing seventy there is a tinge of the usually
unseen miraculous when you wake up alive
from a night's sleep or a nap. We always rise in the terrifying
posture of the living. Some days the river is incomprehensible.
No, not the posture, but that a terrifying beauty
is born within us. I think of the twenty-acre thicket
my mother planted after the deaths forty years ago,
the thicket now nearly impenetrable as its own beauty.
Across the small pond the green heron looked at me quizzically —
who is this? I said I wasn't sure at that moment
wondering if the green heron could be Mother.

—

Now back in the Absarokas I'm awake
to these diffuse corridors of light. The grizzlies
have buried themselves below that light cast down
across the mountain meadow, following a canyon
to the valley floor where the rattlesnakes will also sleep
until mid-April. Meanwhile we'll travel toward the border
with the birds. The moon is swollen tonight

and the mountain this summer I saw bathed
in a thunderstorm now bathes itself in a mist of snow.

—

Rushing, turbulent water and light, convinced by animals
and rivers that nature only leads us to herself,
so openly female through the window of my single eye.
For half a year my alphabet blinded me to beauty,
forgetting my nature which came from the boy lost
comfortably in the woods, how and why he suspected home,
this overmade world where old paths are submerged
in metal and cement.

—

This morning in the first clear sunlight making its way
over the mountains, the earth covered with crunchy frost,
I walked the dogs past Weber's sheep pasture
where a ram was covering a ewe who continued eating,
a wise and experienced woman. I headed due west
up the slope toward Antelope Butte in the delicious
cold still air, turning at the irrigation ditch hearing
the staccato howl of sandhill cranes behind me,
a couple of hundred rising a mile away from Cargill's
alfalfa, floating up into the white mist rising
from the frost, and moving north in what I judge
is the wrong direction for this weather. Birds make mistakes,
so many dying against windows and phone wires.
I continued west toward the snake den to try to catch
the spirit of the place when it's asleep, the sheer otherness
of hundreds of rattlesnakes sleeping in a big ball
deep in the rocky earth beneath my feet. The dogs,
having been snake trained, are frightened of this place.
So am I. So much protective malevolence. I fled.
Back home in the studio, a man-made wonder. We planted

a chokecherry tree near the window and now through cream-
colored blinds the precise silhouette of the bare branches,
gently but firmly lifting my head, a Chinese screen
that no one made which I accept from the nature of light.

—

I think of Mother's thicket as her bird garden.
How obsessed she was with these creatures. When I told
her a schizophrenic in Kentucky wrote, "Birds are holes
in heaven through which a man may pass," her eyes teared.
She lost husband and daughter to the violence of the road
and I see their spirits in the bird garden. On our last night
a few years ago she asked me, "Are we the same species as God?"
At eighty-five she was angry that the New Testament wasn't fair
to women and then she said, "During the Great Depression
we had plenty to eat," meaning at the farmhouse,
barn and chicken coop a hundred yards to the north
that are no longer there, disappeared with the inhabitants.
The child is also the mother of the man.

—

In the U.P. in the vast place southeast of the river
I found my way home by following the path
where my shadow was the tallest
which led to the trail which led
to another trail which led to the road home
to the cabin where I wrote to her:
"Found two dead redtail hawks, missing
their breasts, doubtless a goshawk took them
as one nests just north of here a half mile
in a tall hemlock on the bend of the river."

—

With only one eye I've learned
to celebrate vision, the eye a painter,
the eye a monstrous fleshy camera
which can't stop itself in the dark
where it sees its private imagination.
The tiny eye that sees the cosmos overhead.

—

Last winter I lost heart between each of seven cities.
Planes never land with the same people who boarded.

—

Walking Mary and Zilpha every morning I wonder
how many dogs are bound by regret
because they are captured by our imaginations
and affixed there by our need to have them do
as we wish when their hearts are quite otherwise.

—

I hope to define my life, whatever is left,
by migrations, south and north with the birds
and far from the metallic fever of clocks,
the self staring at the clock saying, "I must do this."
I can't tell the time on the tongue of the river
in the cool morning air, the smell of the ferment
of greenery, the dust off the canyon's rock walls,
the swallows swooping above the scent of raw water.

—

Maybe we're not meant to wake up completely.
I'm trying to think of what I can't remember.
Last week in France I read that the Ainu in Japan
receive messages from the gods through willow trees,
so I'm not the only one. I looked down into the garden

of Matignon and wondered at the car trip the week before
where at twilight in Narbonne 27,000 blackbirds swirled,
and that night from the window
it was eerie with a slip of the waning moon
off the right shoulder of the Romanesque cathedral
with Venus sparkling shamelessly above the moon,
Venus over whom the church never had any power.
Who sees? Whose eye is this? A day later in Collioure
from the Hermitage among vineyards in the mountains
I could look down steep canyons still slightly green
from the oaks in November to the startling blue of the Mediterranean,
storm-wracked from the mistral's seventy-knot winds,
huge lumpy whitecaps, their crests looking toward Africa.

—

I always feared losing my remaining eye,
my singular window to the world. When closed it sees
the thousands of conscious photos I've taken with it,
impressionist rather than crystalline, from a lion's mouth
in the Serengeti in 1972 to a whale's eye in the Humboldt current,
to the mountain sun gorged with the color of forest
fires followed by a moon orange as a simple orange,
a thousand girls and women I've seen but never met,
the countless birds I adopted since losing the eye in 1945
including an albino grouse creamy as that goshawk's breast
that came within feet of Mother in our back pasture,
the female trogon that appeared when Dalva
decided to die, and the thousands of books out of whose print
vision is created in the mind's eye, as real as any garden at dawn.

—

No rhapsodies today. Home from France
and the cold wind and a foot of snow have destroyed
my golden window, but then the memory

has always been more vivid than the life. The memory
is the not-quite-living museum of our lives.
Sometimes its doors are insufferably wide open
with black stars in a gray sky, and horses
clattering in and out, our dead animals resting here
and there but often willing to come to life again
to greet us, parents and brothers and sisters sitting
at the August table laughing while they eat twelve
fresh vegetables from the garden. Rivers, creeks, lakes
over which birds funnel like massive schools of minnows.
In memory the clocks have drowned themselves, leaving
time to the life spans of trees. The world of our lives
comes unbidden as night.

ADVICE

A ratty old man, an Ojibwe alcoholic who lived to be eighty-eight
and chewed Red Man tobacco as a joke, told me a few years back that
time lasted seven times longer than we "white folks" think. This irri-
tated me. We were sitting on the porch of his shack drinking a bot-
tle of Sapphire gin that I brought over. He liked expensive gin. An
old shabby-furred bear walked within ten feet of us on the way to
the bird feeder for a mouthful of sunflower seed. "That bear was a
pissant as a boy. He'd howl in my window until I made him popcorn
with bacon grease. You should buy a green Dodge from the fifties, a
fine car but whitewash it in the late fall, and scrub it off May 1. Never
drive the highways, take back roads. The Great Spirit made dirt not
cement and blacktop. On your walks in the backcountry get to where
you're going, then walk like a heron or sandhill crane. They don't
miss a thing. Study turtles and chickadees. These bears and wolves
around here have too much power for us to handle right. I used to
take naps near a female bear who farted a lot during blueberry sea-
son. Always curtsey to the police and they'll leave you alone. They
don't like to deal with what they can't figure out. Only screw fatter
women because they feed you better. This skinny woman over near
Munising gave me some crunchy cereal that cut my gums. A bigger
woman will cook you ham and eggs. I've had my .22 Remington sev-
enty years and now it looks like it's made out of duct tape. Kerosene
is your best fuel. If you row a boat you can't help but go in a circle.
Once I was so cold and hungry I ate a hot deer heart raw. I felt its last
beat in my mouth. Sleep outside as much as you can but don't close
your eyes. I had this pet garter snake that lived in my coat pocket
for three years. She would come out at night and eat the flies in my
shack. Think of your mind as a lake. Give away half the money you
make or you'll become a bad person. During nights of big moons try
walking as slow as a skunk. You'll like it. Don't ever go in a basement.
Now I see Teddy's fish tug coming in. If you buy a six-pack I'll get

us a big lake trout from Teddy. I got three bucks burning a hole in my pocket. Women like their feet rubbed. Bring them wildflowers. My mom died when I was nine years old. I got this idea she became a bird and that's why I talk to birds. Way back then I thought the Germans and Japs would kill the world but here we are about ready to cook a fish. What more could you want on an August afternoon?"

FIBBER

My bird-watching friends tell me, "You're always seeing birds that don't exist." And I answer that my eye seems to change nearly everything it sees and is also drawn to making something out of nothing, a habit since childhood. I'm so unreliable no one asks me, "What's that?" knowing that a sandhill crane in a remote field can become a yellow Volkswagen. In moments, the girl's blue dress becomes the green I prefer. Words themselves can adopt confusing colors, which can become a burden while reading. You don't have to become what you already are, which is a relief. Today in Sierra Vista while carrying six plastic bags of groceries I fell down. Can that be a curb? What else? The ground rushed up and I looked at gravel inches away, a knee and hands leaking blood. Time and pain are abstractions you can't see but you know when they're with you like a cold hard wind. It's time to peel my heart off my sleeve. It sits there red and glistening like a pig's heart on Grandpa's farm in 1947 and I have to somehow get it back into my body.

There was a terrible mistake when I checked my driver's license today and saw that I'd be seventy next week. At 3:30 a.m. I was only ten and heard Dad with that coal shovel on a cool May morning in the basement, his steps on the stairs, then he woke me for trout fishing with scrambled eggs, a little coffee in my milk, and then we were off in the car, a '47 Chevy two-tone, blue and beige, for the Pine River about an hour's distance up through Luther, the two-track off the county road muddy so he gunned it. He settled me near a deep hole in the bend of the river and then headed upstream to his favorite series of riffle corners. The water was a little muddy and streamer flies didn't work so I tied on a bright Colorado spinner and a gob of worms. In the next four hours I caught three good-sized suckers and three small brown trout. I kept the trout for our second break-fast and let the suckers go. It was slow enough that I felt lucky that I'd brought along a couple dozen Audubon cards to check out birds. Back then I wanted to see a yellow-bellied sapsucker and I still do. While I dozed I hooked my biggest brown trout, about two pounds, and wished I had been awake. When Dad came back downstream and started a small fire I fibbed about my heroism catching the trout, a lifelong habit. He fried the fish with bacon grease stored in a baby food jar. He cut up a quarter-loaf of Mother's Swedish rye bread and we ate the fish with the bread, salt and pepper. Dad napped and I walked back into the dense swampy woods getting a little lost until he called out after waking. Midafternoon we packed up to leave with a creel full of trout for the family and I left my fly rod in the grass behind the car and Dad backed over it. I had paid ten bucks for it earned at fifteen cents an hour at lawn and garden work. Dad said, "Get your head out of your ass, Jimmy." They're still saying that.

COLD WIND

I like those old movies where tires and wheels run backwards on
horse-drawn carriages pursued by Indians, or Model A's driven by
thugs leaning out windows with tommy guns ablaze. Of late I feel a
cold blue wind through my life and need to go backwards myself to
the outback I once knew so well where there were too many mos-
quitoes, blackflies, curious bears, flowering berry trees of sugar plum
and chokeberry, and where sodden and hot with salty sweat I'd slide
into a cold river and drift along until I floated against a warm sandbar,
thinking of driving again the gravel backroads of America at thirty-
five miles per hour in order to see the ditches and gulleys, the birds
in the fields, the mountains and rivers, the skies that hold our 10,000
generations of mothers in the clouds waiting for us to fall back into
their arms again.

ALIEN

It was one of those mornings when my feet seemed unaware of each other and I walked slowly up a canyon wash to avoid tripping. It was warmish at dawn but the sun wouldn't quite come out, having missed a number of good chances, or so I thought studying the antic clouds that were behaving as sloppily as the government. I was looking for a wildflower, the penstemon, but stopped at a rock pool in a miniature marsh seeing a Mojave rattlesnake curled up in the cup of a low-slung boulder. Since this snake can kill a cow or horse I detoured through a dense thicket then glimpsed the small opening of a side canyon I had not noticed in my seventeen years of living down the road. How could I have missed it except that it's my habit to miss a great deal? And then the sun came out and frightened me as if I had stumbled onto a well-hidden house of the gods, roofless and only a hundred feet long, backed by a sheer wall of stone. I smelled the telltale urine of a mountain lion but no cave was visible until I looked up at a passing Mexican jay who shrieked the usual warning. We move from fear to fear. I knew the lion would be hiding there in the daytime more surely than I had seen the snake. They weren't guardians. This is where they lived. These small rock cathedrals are spread around the landscape in hundreds of variations but this one had the rawness of the unseen, giving me an edge of discomfort rarely felt in nature except in Ecuador and the Yucatán where I had appeared as a permanent stranger. I sat down with my back tight against a sheer wall thinking that the small cave entrance I faced by craning my neck must be the home of the old female lion seen around here not infrequently and that she could only enter from a crevasse at the top, downward into her cave. This is nature without us. This is someone's home where I don't belong.

Maybe the problem is that I got involved with the wrong crowd
of gods when I was seven. At first they weren't harmful and only
showed themselves as fish, birds, especially herons and loons, turtles,
a bobcat and a small bear, but not deer and rabbits who only offered
themselves as food. And maybe I spent too much time inside the
water of lakes and rivers. Underwater seemed like the safest church
I could go to. And sleeping outside that young might have seeped
too much dark into my brain and bones. It was not for me to ever
recover. The other day I found a quarter in the driveway I lost at the
Mecosta County Fair in 1947 and missed out on five rides including
the Ferris wheel and the Tilt-A-Whirl. I sat in anger for hours in the
bull barn mourning my lost quarter on which the entire tragic his-
tory of earth is written. I looked up into the holes of the bulls' mas-
sive noses and at the brass rings puncturing their noses which allowed
them to be led. It would have been an easier life if I had allowed a
ring in my nose, but so many years later I still find the spore of the
gods here and there but never in the vicinity of quarters.

Songs of Unreason

| 2011

BROOM

To remember you're alive
visit the cemetery of your father
at noon after you've made love
and are still wrapped in a mammalian
odor that you are forced to cherish.
Under each stone is someone's inevitable
surprise, the unexpected death
of their biology that struggled hard, as it must.
Now to home without looking back,
enough is enough.
En route buy the best wine
you can afford and a dozen stiff brooms.
Have a few swallows then throw the furniture
out the window and begin sweeping.
Sweep until the walls are
bare of paint and at your feet sweep
until the floor disappears. Finish the wine
in this field of air, return to the cemetery
in evening and wind through the stones
a slow dance of your name visible only to birds.

NOTATION

They say the years are layers, laminae.
They lie. Our minds aren't stuck together
like trees. We're much nearer to a ball of snakes
in winter, a flock of blackbirds, a school of fish.
Your brain guides you away from sentences.
It is consoled by the odor of the chokecherry tree
that drifts its sweetness through the studio window.
Chokecherry trees have always been there
along with crab apples. The brain doesn't care
about layers. It is both vertical and horizontal
in a split second, in all directions at once.
Nearly everything we are taught is false
except how to read. All these poems that drift
upward in our free-floating minds hang there
like stationary birds with a few astonishing
girls and women. Einstein lights a cigarette
and travels beyond the galaxies that have
no layers. Our neurons are designed after 90 billion galaxies.
As a shattered teenager I struggled to paint
a copy of El Greco's *View of Toledo* to Berlioz's Requiem.
The canvas was too short but very deep. I walked
on my knees to see what the world looked like
to Toulouse-Lautrec. It didn't work. I became seven
again. It was World War II. I was about
to lose an eye. The future was still in the sky
above me, which I had to learn to capture
in the years that never learned as clouds
to be layered. First warm day. Chokecherry burst. Its song.

POET WARNING

He went to sea
in a thimble of poetry
without sail or oars
or anchor. What chance
do I have, he thought?
Hundreds of thousands
of moons have drowned out here
and there are no gravestones.

A PUZZLE

I see today that everyone on earth
wants the answer to the same question
but none has the language to ask it.
The inconceivable is clearly the inconceivable.
Bum mutter, teethchatter, brain flotsam,
we float up from our own depths
to the sky not the heavens, an invention
of the murderers. Dogs know the answer
by never asking the question but can't advise us.
Here is the brain that outran the finish line:
on a dark day when the world was slate
the yellow sun blasted the mountain across
the river so that it flung its granitic light
in the four directions to which we must bow.
Life doesn't strangle on ironies, we made
that part up. Close after dawn the sheep next door
leave their compound, returning at twilight.
With the rains this was a prodigious green year,
and now the decay of autumn sleeps in dead comfort.
Words are moving water—muddy, clear, or both.

RUMINATION

I sit up late dumb as a cow,
which is to say
somewhat conscious with thirst
and hunger, an eye for the new moon
and the morning's long walk
to the water tank. Everywhere
around me the birds are waiting
for the light. In this world of dreams
don't let the clock cut up
your life in pieces.

ORIOLE

Emerging after three months to the edge
of the hole of pain I arrange
ten orange halves on a stiff wire
off the patio between a small tree
and the feeder. Early next morning
five orioles of three species appear:
Scott's, hooded, Bullock's. Thinking
of those long nights: this is what agony wanted,
these wildly colored birds to inhabit
my mind far from pain.
Now they live inside me.

RIVER II

Another dawn in the village by the river
and I'm jealous of the 63 moons of Jupiter.
Out in the yard inspecting a lush lilac bush
followed by five dogs who have chosen
me as their temporary leader. I look up
through the vodka jangle of the night before,
straight up at least 30,000 feet where the mountains
are tipping over on me. Dizzy I grab the lilacs
for support. Of course it's the deceitful clouds
playing the game of becoming mountains.
Once on our nighttime farm on a moonlit walk
the clouds pushed by a big western wind
became a school of whales swimming hard
across the cold heavens and I finally knew
that we walk the bottom of an ocean we call sky.

RIVER V

Resting in an eddy against dense greenery
so thick you can't see into it but can fathom
its depth by waning birdcalls, hum of insects.
This morning I learned that we live and die
as children to the core only carrying
as a protective shell a fleshy costume
made up mostly of old scar tissue
from before we learned how to protect ourselves.
It's hard to imagine that this powerful
river had to begin with a single drop
far into the mountains, a seep or trickle
from rocks and then the runoff from snowmelt.
Of course watershed means the shedding
of water, rain, a hundred creeks, a thousand
small springs. My mind can't quite
contain this any more than my own inception
in a single sperm joining a single egg
utterly invisible, hidden in Mother's moist
dark. Out of almost nothing, for practical
purposes nothing, then back as ancient
children to the great nothing again,
the song of man and water moving to the ocean.

RIVER VI

I thought years ago that old Heraclitus was wrong.
You can't step into the same river even once.
The water slips around your foot like liquid time
and you can't dry it off after its passage.
Don't bother taking your watch to the river,
the moving water is a glorious second hand.
Properly understood the memory loses nothing
and we humans are never allowed to let our minds
sit on the still bank and have a simple picnic.
I had an unimaginable dream when young
of being a river horse that could easily plunge upstream.
Perhaps it came from our huge black mare June
whom I rode bareback as she swam the lake
in big circles, always getting out where she got in.
Meanwhile this river is surrounded by mountains
covered with lodgepole pines that are mortally diseased,
browning in the summer sun. Everyone knows
that lightning will strike and Montana burn.
We all stay quiet about it, this blessed oxygen
that makes the world a crematory. Only the water is safe.

GRAND MARAIS

The wind came up so strongly at midnight
the cabin creaked in its joints and between
the logs, the tin roof hummed and shuddered
and in the woods you could hear the dead
trees called widow-makers falling
with staccato crashes, and by 3 a.m.
the thunderous roar of Lake Superior miles away.
My dog Rose comes from the sofa
where she invariably sleeps. Her face is close
to mine in the dark, a question on her breath.
Will the sun rise again? She gets on the bed trembling.
I wonder what the creature life is doing
without shelter? Rose is terribly frightened
of this lordly old bear I know who visits
the yard for the sunflower seeds I put out
for the birds. I placed my hand on his head one night
through the car window when I was drunk.
He doesn't give a shit about violent storms
knowing the light comes from his mind, not the sun.

DEBTORS

They used to say we're living on borrowed
time but even when young I wondered
who loaned it to us? In 1948 one grandpa
died stretched tight in a misty oxygen tent,
his four sons gathered, his papery hand
grasping mine. Only a week before, we were fishing.
Now the four sons have all run out of borrowed time
while I'm alive wondering whom I owe
for this indisputable gift of existence.
Of course time is running out. It always
has been a creek heading east, the freight
of water with its surprising heaviness
following the slant of the land, its destiny.
What is lovelier than a creek or riverine thicket?
Say it is an unknown benefactor who gave us
birds and Mozart, the mystery of trees and water
and all living things borrowing time.
Would I still love the creek if I lasted forever?

DEATH AGAIN

Let's not get romantic or dismal about death.
Indeed it's our most unique act along with birth.
We must think of it as cooking breakfast,
it's that ordinary. Break two eggs into a bowl
or break a bowl into two eggs. Slip into a coffin
after the fluids have been drained, or better yet,
slide into the fire. Of course it's a little hard
to accept your last kiss, your last drink,
your last meal about which the condemned
can be quite particular as if there could be
a cheeseburger sent by God. A few lovers
sweep by the inner eye, but it's mostly a placid
lake at dawn, mist rising, a solitary loon
call, and staring into the still, opaque water.
We'll know as children again all that we are
destined to know, that the water is cold
and deep, and the sun penetrates only so far.

Dead Man's Float

| 2016

SOLSTICE LITANY

1

The Saturday morning meadowlark
came in from high up
with her song gliding into tall grass
still singing. How I'd like
to glide around singing in the summer
then to go south to where I already was
and find fields full of meadowlarks
in winter. But when walking my dog
I want four legs to keep up with her
as she thunders down the hill at top speed
then belly flops into the deep pond.
Lark or dog I crave the impossible.
I'm just human. All too human.

2

I was nineteen and mentally
infirm when I saw the prophet Isaiah.
The hem of his robe was as wide
as the horizon and his trunk and face
were thousands of feet up in the air.
Maybe he appeared because I had read him
so much and opened too many ancient doors.
I was cooking my life in a cracked clay
pot that was leaking. I had found
secrets I didn't deserve to know.
When the battle for the mind is finally
over it's late June, green and raining.

3

A violent windstorm the night before
the solstice. The house creaked and yawned.
I thought the morning might bring a bald earth,
bald as a man's bald head but not shiny.
But dawn was fine with a few downed trees,
the yellow rosebush splendidly intact.
The grass was all there dotted with Black
Angus cattle. The grass is indestructible
except to fire but now it's too green to burn.
What did the cattle do in this storm?
They stood with their butts toward the wind,
erect Buddhists waiting for nothing in particular.
I was in bed cringing at gusts,
imagining the contents of earth all blowing
north and piled up where the wind stopped,
the pile sky-high. No one can climb it.
A gopher comes out of a hole as if nothing happened.

4

The sun should be a couple of million miles
closer today. It wouldn't hurt anything
and anyway this cold rainy June is hard
on me and the nesting birds. My own nest
is stupidly uncomfortable, the chair
of many years. The old windows don't keep
the weather out, the wet wind whipping
my hair. A very old robin drops dead
on the lawn, a first for me. Millions
of birds die but we never see it—they like
privacy in this holy, fatal moment or so
I think. We can't tell each other when we die.

Others must carry the message to and fro.
"He's gone," they'll say. While writing an average poem
destined to disappear among the millions of poems
written now by mortally average poets.

5

Solstice at the cabin deep in the forest.
The full moon shines in the river, there are pale
green northern lights. A huge thunderstorm
comes slowly from the west. Lightning strikes
a nearby tamarack bursting into flame.
I go into the cabin feeling unworthy.
At dawn the tree is still smoldering
in this place the gods touched earth.

ANOTHER COUNTRY

I love these raw moist dawns with
a thousand birds you hear but can't
quite see in the mist.
My old alien body is a foreigner
struggling to get into another country.
The loon call makes me shiver.
Back at the cabin I see a book
and am not quite sure what that is.

SEVEN IN THE WOODS

Am I as old as I am?
Maybe not. Time is a mystery
that can tip us upside down.
Yesterday I was seven in the woods,
a bandage covering my blind eye,
in a bedroll Mother made me
so I could sleep out in the woods
far from people. A garter snake glided by
without noticing me. A chickadee
landed on my bare toe, so light
she wasn't believable. The night
had been long and the treetops
thick with a trillion stars. Who
was I, half-blind on the forest floor
who was I at age seven? Sixty-eight
years later I can still inhabit that boy's
body without thinking of the time between.
It is the burden of life to be many ages
without seeing the end of time.

THE PRESENT

I'm sitting on the lip of this black hole, a well
that descends to the center of the earth.
With a big telescope aimed straight down
I see a red dot of fire and hear the beast howling.
My back is suppurating with disease,
the heart lurches left and right,
the brain sings its ditties.
Everywhere blank white movies wait to be seen.
The skylark flew within inches of the rocks
before it stopped and rose again.
The cost of flight is landing.

A VARIATION ON MACHADO

I worry much about the suffering
of Machado. I was only one when he carried
his mother across the border from Spain to France
in a rainstorm. She died and so did he
a few days later in a rooming house along a dry canal.
To carry Mother he abandoned a satchel
holding his last few years of poetry.
I've traveled to Collioure several times
to search for Machado's lost satchel.
The French fed him but couldn't save him.
There's no true path to a death –
we discover the path by walking.
We turn a corner on no road
and there's a house on a green hill
with a thousand colorful birds sweeping in a circle.
Are the poems in the basement of the house on the hill?
We'll find out if we remember earth at all.

LORCA AGAIN

When Lorca was murdered
they had him turn around and look down
the steep mountainside at Granada far below.
Goodbye hometown. They shot him in the back as always,
also in the butt because he was gay. The powerful
rifles splintered him and later the family
picked up the pieces on the slope for burial.
What a rare bird. It was like shooting
the last blue heron on earth. There's a sundial
there now. We drank a bottle Christine made
called *Memoire*. I choked on the wine
and tears. At some ages he was my favorite
poet who would make me moonstruck.
I walked along the Guadalquivir in Seville
and saw his perpetual shadow in the moving
water, the local *gitano* music constricting
and exploding the heart. Water kept carrying
this burden of musical shadow to the ocean.
In the Mediterranean I heard his voice on the water.

FEBRUARY

Warm enough here in Patagonia AZ to read
the new Mandelstam outside in my underpants
which is to say he was never warm enough
except in summer and he was without paper to write
and his belly was mostly empty most of the time
like that Mexican girl I picked up on a mountain road
the other day who couldn't stop weeping. She had slept
out two nights in a sweater in below-freezing weather.
She had been headed to Los Angeles but the *coyote*
took her money and abandoned her in the wilderness.
Her shoes were in pieces and her feet bleeding.
I took her to town and bought her food. She got a ride
to Nogales. She told us in Spanish that she just wanted
to go home and sleep in her own bed. That's what Mandelstam
wanted with mother in the kitchen fixing dinner. Everyone
wants this. Mandelstam said, "To be alone is to be alive."
"Lost and looked in the sky's asylum eye." "What of
her nights?" Maybe she was watched by some of the fifty
or so birds I have in the yard now. When they want to
they just fly away. I gave them my yard and lots of food.
They smile strange bird smiles. She couldn't fly away.
Neither can I though I've tried a lot lately to migrate
to the Camargue on my own wings. When they are married,
Mandelstam and the Mexican girl, in heaven they'll tell
long stories of the horrors of life on earth ending each session
by chanting his beautiful poems that we did not deserve.

APPLE TREE

Sitting under the apple tree on a hot
June day harassed by blackbirds
and a house wren who have nests there.
I'm thinking of the future and the past,
and how the past at my age has become
obviously so much longer than the future.
This feeling always precedes my sense
that severe weather is coming. I don't believe
in doom or destiny—I believe in turmoil,
thunderstorms in the head, rolling lightning
coming down my brain's road. As an artist
you follow the girl in the white tennis dress
for 25,000 miles and never close the deal.

GALACTIC

Sitting out in my chair near Linda's garden.
A mixture of flowers and vegetables, pink iris,
wild poppies, roses, blue salvia and veronica
among tomatoes, green beans, eggplant and onion.
I think that I sense the far-flung galaxies
and hear a tinge of the solar winds.
Where is my dead brother? I want to know.
With so many infirmities I await the miraculous.
Galaxies are grand thickets of stars
in which we may hide forever.

WARBLER

This year we have two gorgeous
yellow warblers nesting in the honeysuckle bush.
The other day I stuck my head in the bush.
The nestlings weigh one-twentieth of an ounce,
about the size of a honeybee. We stared at
each other, startled by our existence.
In a month or so, when they reach the size
of bumblebees they'll fly to Costa Rica without a map.

BRIDGE

Most of my life was spent
building a bridge out over the sea
though the sea was too wide.
I'm proud of the bridge
hanging in the pure sea air. Machado
came for a visit and we sat on the
end of the bridge, which was his idea.

Now that I'm old the work goes slowly.
Ever nearer death, I like it out here
high above the sea bundled
up for the arctic storms of late fall,
the resounding crash and moan of the sea,
the hundred-foot depth of the green troughs.
Sometimes the sea roars and howls like
the animal it is, a continent wide and alive.
What beauty in this the darkest music
over which you can hear the lightest music of human
behavior, the tender connection between men and galaxies.

So I sit on the edge, wagging my feet above
the abyss. Tonight the moon will be in my lap.
This is my job, to study the universe
from my bridge. I have the sky, the sea, the faint
green streak of Canadian forest on the far shore.

Jim Harrison (1937–2016) was one of those rare American writers who made his living *as* a writer. He authored more than three dozen books—all of which remain in print—and his literary work has been translated into two dozen languages. In the late 1970s, Harrison published the novella trilogy *Legends of the Fall*. The success of *Legends* led to his work in Hollywood writing screenplays. Known also for his deep appreciation of food and drink, Harrison wrote popular food columns for *Esquire* and *Brick*.

As a young poet he coedited *Sumac* magazine with fellow poet Dan Gerber and also earned a Guggenheim Fellowship. In 2007, he was elected to the Academy of American Arts and Letters. His extensive literary archive is housed at Grand Valley State University, and *Jim Harrison: A Comprehensive Bibliography* was published by University of Nebraska Press in 2009.

Jim Harrison was fiercely loyal to independent publishers, and two independent publishers are particularly loyal to his work: Grove Atlantic is dedicated to publishing Harrison's fiction and nonfiction, and Copper Canyon Press is committed to his poetry. As the *Sunday Times of London* wrote, "Jim Harrison is a writer with immortality in him."

Joseph Bednarik, copublisher of Copper Canyon Press, served as Jim Harrison's poetry editor since the late 1990s. He is also the coeditor of *One-Man Boat: The George Hitchcock Reader* and *The Sumac Reader*.

INDEX OF TITLES

Poetry is vital to language and living. Since 1972, Copper Canyon Press has published extraordinary poetry from around the world to engage the imaginations and intellects of readers, writers, booksellers, librarians, teachers, students, and donors.

WE ARE GRATEFUL FOR THE MAJOR SUPPORT PROVIDED BY:

THE PAUL G. ALLEN
FAMILY FOUNDATION

The Chinese character for poetry is made up of two parts: "word" and "temple." It also serves as pressmark for Copper Canyon Press.

This book is set in Bembo Book MT Pro with display heads set in Arno Headline and Display. Book design by VJBScribe. Printed on archival-quality paper.